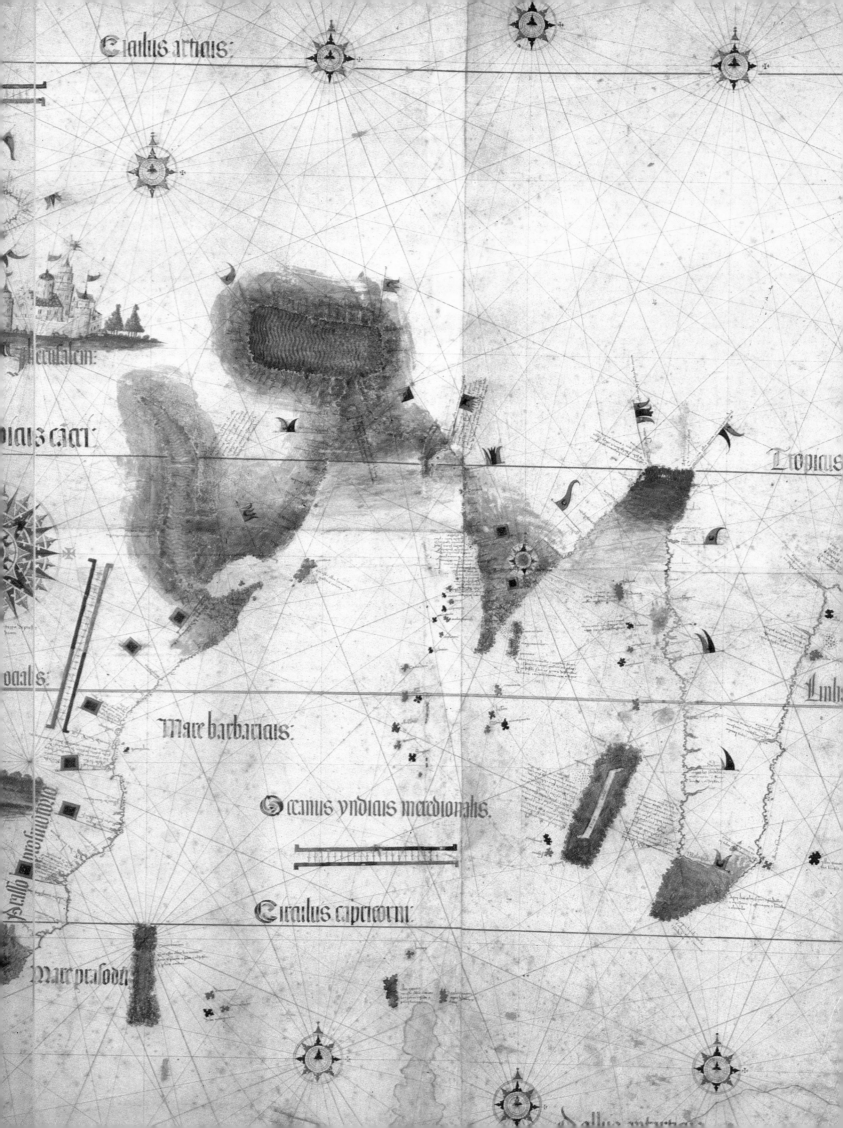

ATLAS OF
WORLD HISTORY

WARWICK PRESS

Contents

Published 1982 by Warwick Press,
730 Fifth Avenue, New York, New York 10019.

First published in Great Britain by
Ward Lock Limited 1982.

Copyright © 1982 by Grisewood & Dempsey Ltd.

Printed in Italy by Vallardi Industrie Grafiche.

Library of Congress Catalog Card No. 81-71548

ISBN 0-531-09206-2

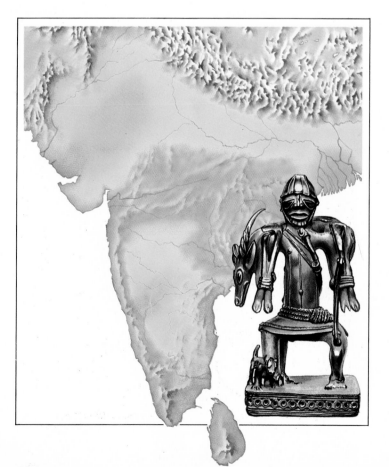

Editorial

Adviser
W. D. Townson

Authors
Anne Millard
Frances Halton

Editor
Frances M. Clapham

Illustrators
Tony Payne
Roger Phillips
Sylvia Goodman
Richard Hook

For Zoë-Louise

The World We Live In

One way in which men have changed the world they live in is by irrigating, or watering, the land so that they can farm it. This Egyptian is using an ox to turn a wheel raising pots of water from a large channel to a smaller one. Methods like this have been used for thousands of years.

People's lives have always been shaped by the places they live in. The food they eat, the clothes they wear, the houses they build, and the work they do all depend on their surroundings. On a larger scale, the histories of nations have been influenced very greatly by the areas in which they live. In this book we look at history and geography together, and see how the countries of today have developed.

The First Settlements

The first people to build villages and towns chose their sites carefully. They needed a good supply of food and water, so they settled on fertile land where it was easy to grow crops, or by a river or the sea where there was plenty of fish to eat. They often chose places which were easy to defend against attack by animals or by neighbouring peoples. Many of them built on top of hills. The early Chinese used rivers to defend at least one side of their towns. The rivers were also a good way of travelling. Many early settlements grew up on trade routes, particularly where two routes crossed.

These first settlements grew larger, and some joined with their neighbours to form states. The ways in which they linked depended a great deal on how easy it was to travel between them. People living on one side of a natural barrier, like a mountain range or a desert, would have little to do with people on the other side. Greek city states were built all around the coasts of the eastern Mediterranean. It was not difficult for the people who lived there to sail across from one to another. Travelling across the mountains inland was far harder. Because of this, the Greeks became very good sailors. They grew rich from carrying goods all over the Mediterranean. More than a thousand years later, the Portuguese had become excellent sailors. They sailed from their poor and barren country to the East, hoping to become rich through trading there. When they reached the East, they built up a great empire there.

Some countries lie on the crossroads of several trade routes, or in places which are easy to travel across. This often gives them a very troubled history. The Bible Lands – Palestine, Syria, and the Lebanon

– lie on the way from Mesopotamia and Anatolia to Egypt. They grew rich through trade, but they were ruled first by one powerful nation, then by another, as these nations tried to get control of the trade routes and built up empires. Belgium and the Netherlands, lying on the flat north European plain, have been invaded many times and often changed hands between powerful countries.

Changing Surroundings

Places shape people's lives, but people can also do a great deal to shape the places they settle in and make them more convenient. From early times on, they have cleared forests and drained marshes to provide more good farming land. They have dug channels to carry water to their crops, and built dams to store water for the dry seasons. This has helped the land produce more food. But people have also been very destructive. They have cut down forests to provide timber and churned up the land to get rock, coal, and other minerals. Sometimes they have farmed the land so badly that the goodness has gone out of it. And in recent times smoke and dirt from factories and cars, and chemicals used on the land, have poisoned the air, much of the land, rivers, and even part of the sea.

Dates and Problems

When we are studying the past, we often need to know exactly when events happened. For a long time, there was no general way of fixing dates. People writing records might use terms like 'in the tenth year of the reign of King Edward', but this was very inconvenient. Then a system of dating grew up in Europe which was based on Jesus's birth. The years that had passed before he was born are described as years BC, which stands for 'before Christ'. The years after are described by the letters AD, standing for *Anno Domini*, the Latin for 'the year of our Lord'. Muslims take the year in which the Prophet Muhammad went from Mecca to Medina as their year 1.

Since the Christian dating system was worked out, historians have found that Jesus was born earlier than they thought – perhaps in the year 6 BC. This points up one of the great problems of history. New evidence about the past is being found all the time, and it may prove that our ideas about what happened are wrong. This is one reason why a new history book may give quite different information from one written some years ago. Another great problem for people who study the past is that they cannot trust written records. Often the people who wrote them wanted to make sure that their own point of view was the one that would be remembered. They wanted later people to believe that they had been, and done, right. We can never really know what happened long ago. But the past is so interesting that many people spend all their lives trying to find out more about it.

People have polluted the Earth with industrial waste and smoke (above) and used its resources heedlessly. Now they are beginning to move into space; the first men landed on the Moon in 1969 (below). We can only hope that people will not squander the resources of other worlds as they have those of their own.

The Ancient World

The story of the past is often divided into three long periods. The first of these is ancient history. Strictly speaking, it begins when men first learned to write about 5500 years ago. The time before that is known as prehistory. The other two main periods are the Middle Ages, and the modern period.

The first real men lived on Earth about 2 million years ago. We have learned a great deal about them and about the sort of lives they lived by studying their bones, the things they made, and the pictures they painted. Once they learnt how to write things down they left a record of their lives. Piecing together the story of the past becomes much easier.

The earliest writing we know about comes from Mesopotamia, the land lying between the river Tigris and the river Euphrates in the Near East. This was

Alexander the Great, King of Macedon, leads his army into battle. Alexander united the Greeks under his rule and led them to victory over the Persians. Under him and his successors, the Greek language and ways of life were spread all through the Near East.

where one of the first great civilizations grew up. Mesopotamia was part of the Fertile Crescent, a region of good farmland that stretched north up the rivers, and then curved west and south down the eastern coast of the Mediterranean to the river Nile in Egypt. Here another great civilization grew up in early times, and many traders travelled between Mesopotamia and Egypt.

Soon writing spread all through the countries of the Near East and around the coasts of the Mediterranean Sea. Because of this, we know far more about the history of this area than we do about any other part of the world. When people in Europe talk about the Ancient World, they usually mean the lands around the Mediterranean, and the great empires built up there. The greatest of all these was the Roman Empire. It ruled the Mediterranean lands and all western Europe, including part of Britain. The Romans linked their empire with a network of good roads along which armies and merchants could travel quickly and easily. They spread their language, Latin, and their laws and customs all through the Empire. But it was difficult to rule over so great an area. People from outside its borders, known as barbarians, often attacked it. In the end, barbarian tribes invaded the Roman Empire in western Europe. In the year AD 476 the Roman emperor in the West had to give up his throne to a barbarian ruler.

This year marks the end of the period of ancient history. From then on, the countries of the Ancient World developed in different ways. But in other parts of the world there was no such break in history. A great civilization had grown up in China, for example, that carried on for thousands of years. Across the world in America, new civilizations were developing quite independently.

IMPORTANT DATES

BC

30,000	People like us were living in many parts of the world, hunting animals and gathering seeds and berries to eat.
28,000	About this time the first people reached America by crossing a land bridge from Asia. Other people were living round Lake Mungo in Australia by this time.
8000s	Farming began in the Near East.
7000s	The first pottery was made.
3000s	The first cities grew up in Mesopotamia and writing was developed there. In about 3100 Egypt became one kingdom.
2000s	The Minoans of Crete became important traders. People in the Indus Valley built up a great civilization.
2000	At about this time Abraham led his tribe into Canaan.
1750	The Shang Dynasty was founded in China. The cities of the Indus were destroyed about now.
1728	Hammurabi became King of Babylon.
1450	The centres of Crete were destroyed except for Knossos, which was taken over by the Mycenaeans of Greece.
776	The first Olympic Games were held in Greece.
753	The Romans believed Rome was founded in this year.
563	The Buddha was born in India.
559	Cyrus the Great founded the Persian Empire.
551	The great philosopher Confucius was born in China.
510	The last king was driven out of Rome, which became a republic.
508	Democratic government was introduced in Athens.
492	The Persians attacked Athens. This was the beginning of Persia's long and unsuccessful fight to conquer Greece.
336	Alexander the Great became King of Macedon. He soon ruled all Greece, and conquered the Persian Empire.
264	War broke out between Rome and the trading city of Carthage. There were three wars altogether, all won by Rome which in 146 completely destroyed Carthage.
221	The Ch'in Dynasty came to power in China and gave the country its name. Under them the Great Wall of China was completed as a defence against invaders.
202	The Han Dynasty came to power in China.
61	Julius Caesar, the Roman general, won his first major victories. He went on to rule Rome, but was murdered in 44. His great nephew Octavian became the first emperor.
6	Jesus was probably born in this year.

AD

30	Jesus was crucified by order of the Romans.
117	The Roman Empire was at its greatest extent.
286	The Emperor Diocletian divided the Roman Empire in two.
313	The Emperor Constantine allowed Christians to worship freely.
410	The Goths under Alaric sacked the city of Rome.
476	The last Roman emperor in the West gave up his throne to the barbarians.

The First Men

No one knows for certain just how people came into being. But about 2 million years ago some early people were living in Africa. We call them 'men' because they walked upright, as we do, and they made themselves tools of stone. But they looked very different from us. They were shorter and hairier, with heavy brows and huge jaws. They looked rather more like apes than like people.

These early people found food by gathering roots and fruits and seeds, and by hunting animals for meat. Over thousands of years they changed and became more and more like modern people. They learnt how to use fire, and how to make clothes out of animal skins. At some time they began to talk. We learn about them from their bones and from the tools they left behind.

By 30,000 years ago people whose bodies were the same shape as ours were living in many parts of the world. At that time the Earth's climate was colder than it is now, and great herds of animals such as mammoths, caribou, and moose wandered over the icy plains of Europe, Central Asia, and America. Groups of men joined together in hunting parties and drove the animals into ambushes, over cliffs, and into marshes. There they could kill them. Probably people followed the herds as they moved from one grazing ground to another. They would go back to the same places year after year.

Some people lived in shelters made of skin and branches, or of animal bones. Others lived in caves in the rocks. They slept on beds made of animal skins, dried grass, and bracken. They scraped animal skins clean with stone tools, and sewed them into clothes with needles of bone. Bone beads and shells decorated their clothes and were made into necklaces and bracelets.

Some of these people painted wonderful pictures deep inside the caves. They made paints out of coloured earth, and drew with charcoal, working by the light of flickering lamps burning animal fat. Their pictures show the animals they hunted. Perhaps these paintings were part of a magic ceremony to bring the hunters luck.

Changing Lives

About 10,000 years ago the world grew warmer. Some of the big mammals died out, and others moved far north, where it was still cold. In many parts of the world people could go on living the same sort of hunting and food-gathering lives, but in other places people began to learn new skills. Over a very long period of time they gradually learnt how to be farmers.

Farming began independently in many different parts of the world. We know best how it grew up in the Near East. At that time there was a region of good farmland which stretched from Egypt, north up the coast of Palestine, and then curved southwards to Mesopotamia. This region is often called the Fertile Crescent. Wild barley and wheat grew in the area. First men harvested the wild wheat and barley, and then they learnt how to sow the seeds and grow their crops where they wanted. Wild sheep, goats, cattle and pigs roamed about. Men learnt how to keep them in herds.

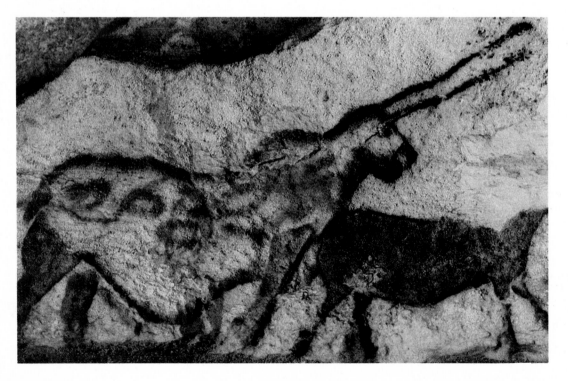

These animals were painted on the walls deep inside a cave at Lascaux in France by hunters who lived from 18,000 to 12,000 years ago. As well as painting the animals they hunted, early men carved them on the walls of caves and made bone figures of them.

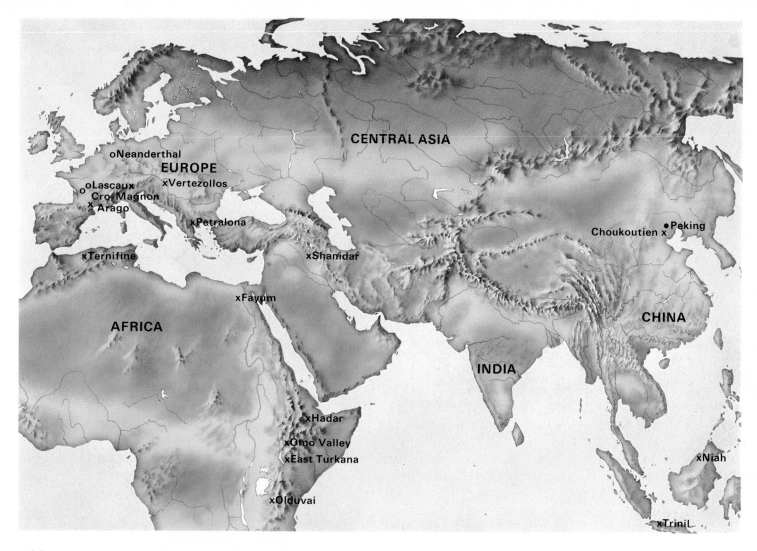

Now people no longer needed to move about in search of food. They could settle down in villages, which they built of local materials – mud bricks in the Near East, and wood in the forests of northern Europe, where people cleared farmland with axes of polished stone. As the animals became tamer, they could be milked and used to carry loads. Wool from the sheep was collected, and soon people learnt how to spin it into thread and weave it into cloth. They shaped pots from clay, and baked them in the fire to make them hard. At first they made tools of flakes of stone, set into wooden handles. Then they discovered how to hammer nuggets of copper into tools, and later how to melt and mix tin and copper to make the hard and strong metal called bronze.

This mammoth tusk has been carved in the shape of two reindeer. It was found in a cave in western France.

This map shows the main areas in which the first men lived. Names marked with x are sites lived in by early forms of people; those marked o show where some of the first truly modern people lived. The man on the left is one of these. The woman below is making a pot from a coil of clay; she lived about 8000 years ago.

13

The Land Between Two Rivers

Mesopotamia means the 'Land between the Two Rivers'. These two rivers are the Tigris and the Euphrates. We call the southern part of ancient Mesopotamia, Sumer. This is a hot, dry place that gets very little rain, but the farmers of Sumer found that if they dug a network of ditches they could store the flood water from the rivers and then let it run into the fields where it was needed. The flood water brought silt which made the fields fertile. This worked so well that the farmers were soon growing more food than their families needed.

The Sumerians used the extra food to support people who had special skills, allowing them to work full time making all the tools, pots, furniture, clothes, jewels, and weapons that were needed. The farmers also paid priests, who knew how to serve the gods and keep them happy. And they paid taxes to kings who ruled them, gave them fair laws, and led them in war. They still had food left over so this and some of the goods made by the craftsmen were sold to foreigners. In return they brought things Sumer lacked, such as stone, wood, and metal.

The First Cities

In this way the Sumerians grew rich, and their numbers increased. By 3200 BC they had started living in great cities, each with its own ruler. The houses were made of mud bricks that had been baked hard in the hot sun. The streets were narrow, but the houses of the rich were comfortable and cool. The

Above: Some of the early people of Sumer lived in the marshes and built huts and boats of reeds, just like these ones built by the people living there today. Wildfowl and pigs living in the marshes, fish from the rivers, and dates all provided them with food.

Left: This mud brick wall, splendidly decorated with a bull, was made by the Babylonians in about 600 BC. Even grand buildings were built of brick, since stone was scarce.

rooms were all grouped round an open courtyard. None of the windows opened on to the street so the dust and noise did not get inside.

Palaces and temple towers called *ziggurats* were also built of mud bricks. A ziggurat had tall platforms built one on top of the other, with a stairway right to the top, where the temple was built. Temples were the homes of the gods and goddesses who guarded the cities and the people. Like most ancient peoples, the Sumerians believed in many gods and goddesses who ruled this world and the Next World after death. The Sumerians made many offerings to keep the gods happy, and the priests held services in their honour. Sumerians believed that kings were sent by the gods to carry out their will on Earth. The kings took a leading role in religious ceremonies such as the great New Year Festival.

In the remains of the city of Ur, archaeologists have found the graves of kings and queens. Their treasure was buried with them. So were a number of their

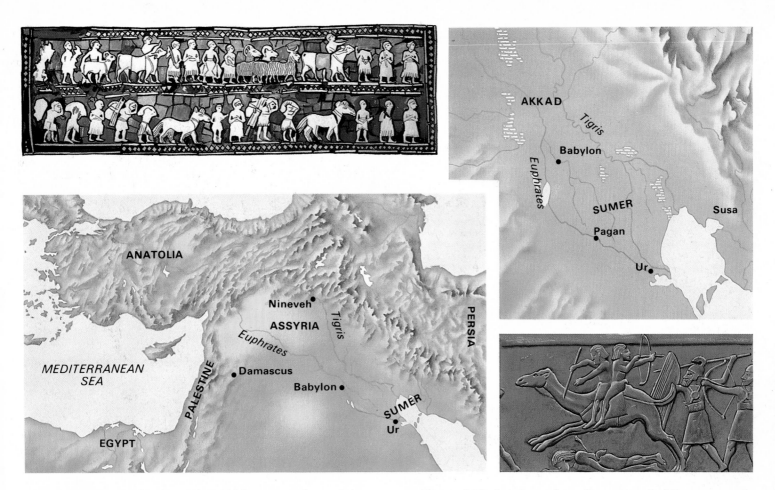

The upper map shows the region of Mesopotamia, and the lower one shows the area around it. The Assyrian empire stretched as far west as Egypt. The picture at the top shows people from the city of Ur in Sumer, in about 2500 BC. Servants drive cattle, sheep, and goats, and labourers carry heavy loads. The figures are made of slivers of red limestone and shell, and the blue bits in the background are lapis lazuli, a blue stone which came from Afghanistan, far to the east. At this time Sumer was a rich and important market, and traders from India and from the Mediterranean visited it. The bottom right picture shows Assyrian warriors. The Assyrians were very warlike and were greatly feared by the peoples over whom they ruled. They carved many huge stone slabs with scenes like this.

servants who would be able to serve their masters in the Next World. Most Sumerians did not look forward to death for they thought the Next World would be a rather dull, miserable place.

Changing Empires

First one, then another Sumerian city grew powerful enough to rule over the others. But about 2350 BC power passed from the cities of Sumer to the land of Akkad to the north. The Akkadians ruled over the first great empire. From now on the ruling power in Mesopotamia changed many times, as different cities or peoples grew stronger. About 1730 Sumer and Akkad were joined under the rule of the kings of Babylon. The most famous early king of Babylon was Hammurabi. He set up a stone pillar on which were written the laws and punishments in force in his day.

About 880 the Assyrians from north Mesopotamia rose to power. They were a cruel, warlike people. They conquered a great empire which included all Mesopotamia, and stretched through Palestine as far as Egypt. They demanded heavy taxes and tributes from the people they ruled. But the Babylonians grew strong once more. They rose in revolt against the Assyrians, and took over their empire in 612. Less than a hundred years later, Babylon itself fell victim to the Persians from the east.

Writing

As they grew wealthy, the Sumerians needed to make records of their goods. At first they drew objects, for example a bull or an ear of wheat, on a clay tablet. As time passed the pictures got more and more simple, until they were just groups of wedge-shaped marks that no longer made pictures. We call this writing *cuneiform*, meaning wedge-shaped. Before long people in many countries in the Near East were writing in cuneiform.

People of Mesopotamia used seals instead of signing letters. This picture shows a sausage-shaped seal and its print. It is in the Elamite language.

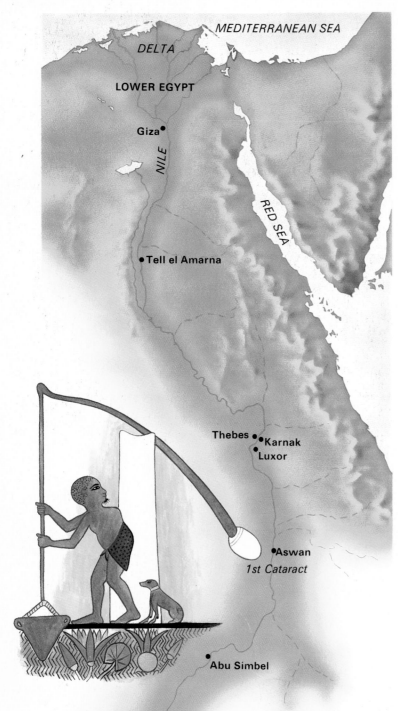

MEDITERRANEAN SEA

DELTA

LOWER EGYPT

Giza

NILE

RED SEA

Tell el Amarna

Thebes
Karnak
Luxor

Aswan
1st Cataract

Abu Simbel

2nd Cataract

The picture above left shows a man using a *shaduf* to raise water. The weight at the end of the curved pole balanced the water in his bucket, which he dipped in the river and then swung round to empty in a smaller channel. Farmers made canals, dykes, and little channels to carry water from the river to their fields.

UPPER EGYPT

3rd Cataract

4th Cataract

5th Cataract

NUBIA

Egypt

Egypt is a very hot dry land, where rain hardly ever falls. Each year, before the modern dams were built, the river Nile flooded the land along its banks. The Ancient Egyptians learnt to store the flood water and take it through canals to their fields. When the Nile flooded, it brought mud as well as water to the fields. This made the soil very good for growing crops. So, as in Mesopotamia, there was plenty of food to spare. Some was stored, in case the next harvest was bad. The rest was sold abroad in exchange for wood, silver, incense, slaves, and many luxuries.

Upper and Lower Kingdoms

Egypt had once been two lands, Upper (south) and Lower (north) Egypt. The lands were united into one kingdom in about 3100 BC, but the kings went on wearing two crowns and calling themselves king of Upper and Lower Egypt. Kings were also believed to be the sons of Ra, the Sun god. The Egyptian king is called the pharaoh. This comes from two Egyptian words *per-o*, meaning Great House – that is, the palace. The Egyptians felt it was not respectful to refer directly to the king, so they said the palace instead.

Dynasties (families of kings) changed and there were some very troubled times, and even invasions by foreigners, but Egypt's way of life went on with little change. Except for a few short spells, it stayed a free land from 3100 to 30 BC, when it became part of the Roman Empire.

The Egyptians were very clever builders. As part of

Egypt stretches for about 1000 kilometres (625 miles) north to south, along the banks of the river Nile. There is little or no rainfall, but every June before the modern dams were built the river flooded, covering the land with rich black mud. This made it very fertile. When the floods went down in September the farmers ploughed and sowed the soil, which was so rich that they could sometimes grow two crops before the really hot season began in April.

In the background of the picture below are the three great pyramids at Giza, built as tombs for pharaohs. They were built in the desert, so that no land which could be farmed was wasted. They are more than 4000 years old, and were one of the Seven Wonders of the Ancient World.

the taxes they owed to the king, peasants worked for him, building temples and his tomb. This was done during the flood season when they could not work on their fields. The Egyptians built their houses and palaces of sun-dried mud bricks, but there was plenty of stone in the desert cliffs on either side of the river valley, so temples and tombs, which were meant to last for ever, were made of stone.

Religion and Death

The statues of Egyptian gods and goddesses, and the carvings of them on temple walls, often show them with the heads of birds or animals. This was because each god had a creature that was very specially linked to him. Everyone knew what a god's own bird or animal was, so if the god was shown with that creature's head even people who could not read the inscription could easily see who he was.

All Egyptians believed that there was a life after death. They loved their land and way of life very much and expected the Next World, ruled over by the god Osiris, to be just like it. This meant that they would go on needing food, drink, clothes, jewels, furniture, and games, so they put all these things in their tombs. The hot, dry sand of the desert where they were buried has preserved the contents of these tombs until the present day. This is why we know so much about how people lived in Ancient Egypt. They painted the tomb walls with scenes of daily life and we can also learn a lot from these pictures.

The Egyptians believed that if you were to enjoy the Next World properly, your earthly body had to survive. So they learnt how to preserve bodies by using special salts and wrapping them in linen bandages. We call this process mummification.

This tomb painting shows people from Africa bringing tribute to the pharaoh. It includes a massive gold chain, and a leopard skin. Gold from Nubia was the source of a great deal of Egypt's wealth. This picture dates from about 1400 BC.

Poor people were buried in holes in the desert sand. People who could afford to, built proper tombs of mud brick or stone, or had tombs cut in the cliffs. Some of the kings built great pyramids for their tombs, but later kings too had tombs cut in the cliffs, in the Valley of the Kings at Thebes. This is where the tomb of King Tutankhamun was found with all his fabulous treasure.

This scene decorates a gold-covered shrine found in the tomb of the pharaoh Tutankhamun. It shows the pharaoh and his queen on a hunting trip.

Above: This little monkey is made of glazed earthenware. Monkeys, like cats and dogs, were popular pets in Egypt.

The Bible Lands

This hillside in Israel has been terraced so that vines can be grown there. Much of Caanan was very fertile, but to the north and east lay deserts. Vines have been cultivated in Canaan for thousands of years, and the Bible often mentions wine and vineyards.

'A land flowing with milk and honey' is how the Bible describes the country to which Moses led the Israelites. This is how Canaan must have seemed to them after their years in the desert, for along the river valleys and the coast there was plenty of grazing for their flocks and herds, and good land for farming too.

The Bible Land of Canaan runs north to south along the east coast of the Mediterranean. Today it is divided up between the states of Israel, Jordan, Lebanon, and Syria. The area of Israel and Jordan is often known as Palestine. In ancient times Canaan lay between two powerful countries. These were Egypt to the south west, and Mesopotamia to the east. Travellers from one to the other had to journey through Canaan, as the more direct way led through desert. Sailors from all over the Mediterranean called in at its ports. The area was a crossroads of trade routes and, often, a battlefield for its powerful neighbours.

Bible Peoples

The Israelites, or Jews as they later became known, were just one of many people living in this area. Many of them, like the Israelites, were wandering herdsmen who moved in from the edge of the desert in search of

good grazing. The Bible tells us that Abraham led in a group of herdsmen (probably in about 2000 BC), and their descendants moved down to Egypt a few hundred years later, again in search of new grazing. The Egyptians quite often let nomadic tribes graze their flocks on the 'Land of Goshen', in the Nile Delta. When Moses led the Israelites back to Canaan they settled down in the hills and valleys west of the river Jordan and began to farm there. They defeated

This painting from an Egyptian tomb, dating from about 1200 BC, shows merchants from Syria with their goods. The trade routes from Mesopotamia and Anatolia to Egypt passed through the Bible Lands.

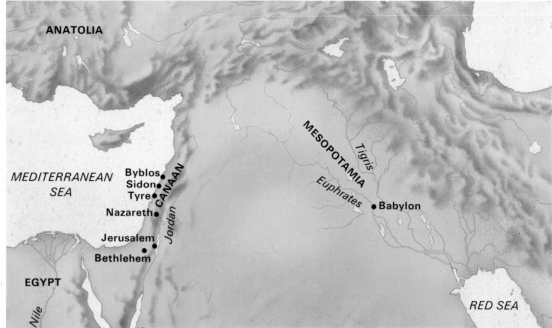

The Bible Lands of the east Mediterranean, and the countries around. Travellers could not cross the deserts of Arabia between Egypt and Mesopotamia, two of the greatest markets of ancient times. Instead they had to journey through Canaan. The ports of Byblos, Tyre, and Sidon belonged to the Phoenicians. They were great traders, and brought goods from all over the Mediterranean. Wood from the Lebanon was taken across country to the Euphrates, and was then floated down river for building palaces.

the people around, and set up a kingdom with its capital at Jerusalem. But to the east great empires were growing up. Assyrians and then Babylonians moved into the area. Many of the people were taken to the great city of Babylon as slaves. They stayed there until it was conquered by the Persians and they were freed. Next the Greeks under Alexander moved in, and when Jesus was born the area was under Roman rule.

Farmers of the Holy Land

When the wandering herdsmen settled down in the valleys and plains of Canaan they became farmers. They sowed their crops of barley or wheat when the rainy season started in October or November. They harvested them in spring. Many vines grew on the hillsides. The grapes were harvested in September. Some were eaten fresh, some were dried in the sun to make raisins, and some were made into wine. Olive trees also grew on the hillsides. Their roots reached deep into the dry ground to find water. The olives were eaten whole or crushed to make oil. This was used for cooking, and as a fuel for lamps.

Sheep and goats were important animals. Often they were grazed together. Donkeys and oxen were used to draw ploughs and carts, and donkeys were used to carry goods. Camels were very useful since they could travel through the desert for several days without food or water. They were not used until about a thousand years before the birth of Jesus.

Judaism and Christianity

Two of the world's greatest religions grew up in the Bible Lands. The first was Judaism, the religion of the Jews. It was different from other early religions, which had many gods. The Jews believed that there was only one God, whom they called Yahweh or

Jehovah, and that he had chosen them to be his people and follow his laws. They also believed that he would send them a saviour, or Messiah, who would rule over God's kingdom. They wrote down God's laws and their history in the Bible.

In about 6 BC Jesus was born in the village of Bethlehem near Jerusalem. When he grew up, he travelled about Canaan, teaching people what God wanted them to do. He said that God's kingdom would not be on Earth, but in the world to come after death. The Jews did not believe that Jesus was the promised Messiah. But many people believed that he was the Messiah, and the Son of God. He was also known as Christ, the Anointed One, and his followers are called Christians. Jesus was killed as a political troublemaker by the Romans. But his followers spread his message all over the world.

A shepherd with his flock in the hills near Hebron. Abraham was a nomad shepherd, wandering with his flocks in search of good grazing, when he led his people into the Bible Lands.

China and India

Farming in China began in the north, on the plains around the Hwang-ho or Yellow River. Here winters are bitterly cold and there is little rain in summer. Sometimes the river floods disastrously. But the fine yellow soil is very fertile and it is easy to grow enough food. Soon farming spread south to the plains of the Yangtze river.

First villages, and then towns grew up along the river banks. Rivers provided water for the fields, and fish to eat. The Chinese built a network of large and small canals, along which boats carried food and people. The farmers grew wheat and millet and barley in the north, and rice in the south where it was hotter. Market gardeners grew vegetables such as melons and onions. They kept pigs and sheep, geese and hens, and planted orchards of fruit trees including apricots and peaches. Oxen were used to pull ploughs and carts.

Village houses were generally built mostly of mud, with tiled roofs. The farmers took much of their produce to local market towns. These were often surrounded by high walls of closely packed earth. Craftsmen had their own special part of the city, where they made pottery and bronze vessels and weapons. They carved ornaments from the precious green stone called jade. Some of these were sent westwards along what became known as the Silk Road, because so much silk cloth was taken from China to the west. For a long time the Chinese were the only people who knew how to produce silk. They could also make paper. They invented a form of money to help them in their trading. At first their coins were many different shapes, but later they were round with a square hole in the middle.

The Chinese Empire

Chinese history begins with the Shang *dynasty* (ruling family) which came to power in about 1500 BC. From then on, Chinese rule and ways of life spread south and west. The vast Chinese Empire was organized by a great army of civil servants. They made sure that laws and taxes, weights and measures were the same all over the Empire. Even the width between cart-wheels had to be the same. The government also controlled two very important industries, the production of salt and the making of iron. Iron-working began in China in the 600s BC; the metal was melted and cast in moulds, not shaped by heating and hammering as in other places. It was another 1800 years before people in Europe began to cast iron!

In other parts of the world, the first great civilizations grew up and then died away. But Chinese civilization developed without a break until the 1900s. Although the ruling families changed and invaders from the north conquered and settled parts of the country, they soon learnt Chinese ways.

Left: The Emperor Kuang-wu, who ruled in the 1st century AD. The emperor of China was known as the Son of Heaven. He was surrounded by servants and lived in great luxury. Below right: Rivers and canals were the most important way of carrying goods from one part of China to another. Many people lived in thatched shelters on the boats.

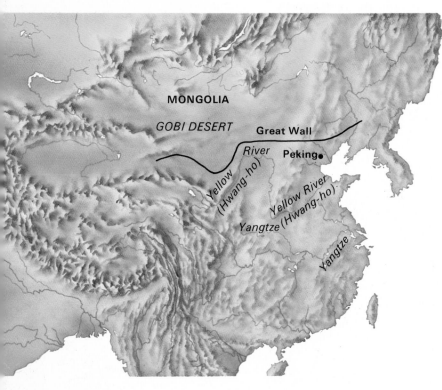

MONGOLIA

GOBI DESERT

Great Wall

Yellow River

Peking

Yellow (Hwang-ho)

Yellow River (Hwang-ho)

Yangtze (Hwang-ho)

Yangtze

A terracotta figure of an oxcart from the Indus Valley.

Peoples of the Indus

In India, people learnt to use the water of the river Indus to make their soil rich and bring them good crops and wealth. The Indus Valley people built a great system of dams and canals. They grew wheat, barley, and cotton and kept animals including buffalo. They may even have had elephants to do the heaviest work. By about 2500 BC they too began to live in cities.

As yet, we cannot read the words written on their little square seals, so we do not have details about their history, laws, kings, and ideas as we have for Mesopotamia and Egypt. All we know about them is what we have found out by digging in their ancient cities. The greatest of the Indus Valley cities found so far are Mohenjo Daro and Harappa, and there were certainly at least a hundred smaller towns and villages.

Streets in the cities were long and straight, and they had covered drains running down the middle to carry off all waste. Comfortable mud brick houses were built round courtyards, each with its own well and a

Two of the world's greatest religions grew up in India. The first was Hinduism, which goes back to well before 1000 BC. It says that there is a single world spirit, Brahman, of which all things are part. It includes many different sorts of gods and beliefs. Hinduism teaches people to obey the divine order of the universe. In the 500s the religion of Buddhism was developed by the great teacher Gautama, who is called the Buddha, the Enlightened One. He taught men certain very important rules. He said that only those who obeyed them could break free from the pain and suffering of life on Earth.

lavatory connected to the drain in the road. These cities had fine public buildings, and two-wheeled ox-carts carried grain to be stored in the city's great granary. Craftsmen carved ivory and worked in gold and copper. Traders from the Indus Valley crossed the mountain passes in the north west and traded with Mesopotamia, as we know from their pottery which has been found there.

The Indus Valley cities lasted about 1000 years, then they were deserted and forgotten. No one knows what happened. In Mohenjo Daro piles of clay missiles were found on the walls. These were probably ammunition for slings. Perhaps the city was attacked. Many unburied bodies were found in the streets. Perhaps they died when the city was taken.

New Arrivals

About the time Mohenjo Daro fell, new people known as Aryans arrived from the north west and settled in northern India. They spread slowly east and south. By about 1000 BC they knew how to work iron, which is a very hard metal and difficult to use. By about this time India itself was divided into many separate kingdoms, each ruled by a fortress-city surrounded by high walls and moats. First one kingdom, then another became powerful enough to rule its neighbours. There were many wars, but most people went on making a living as craftsmen or as farmers on the fertile plains.

The City States of Greece

North west of Egypt lies the Aegean Sea. It is dotted with rocky islands, and on either side are two mountainous countries: mainland Greece on the west, and Anatolia (modern Turkey) on the east. The cities of the Aegean area were built on small pockets of farmland along the coast. The people there grew grain, grapes for wine, and olives. Few people were rich enough to own many cattle or horses, which need good grass. Most farmers kept sheep, goats, and pigs, which are easier to feed. It was easier to travel by sea than overland across the mountains, and the Greeks became good sailors. Soon they came to rely more and more on trading for a living.

The Minoans of Crete

The largest island in the Aegean is Crete. Its people were the first in this area to grow rich. They learnt to make fine pottery and cloth, and later they became expert bronze workers. They traded their wares with Egypt and the other Mediterranean peoples. The people of Crete are known as Minoans, after their legendary King Minos. They built great centres, called palaces, decorated with marvellous paintings. But suddenly, in about 1450 BC, some disaster came to Crete. No one knows what happened, although the

This map shows how the Greek cities were scattered along the coasts and on the islands of the eastern Mediterranean Sea. There were more Greek colonies along the coasts of the Black Sea. There farmers grew good crops of grain, much of which they sent back to their mother cities.

The Greek theatre at Taormina in Sicily. The Greeks were the first people to write plays, which they acted at religious festivals. They built theatres like this in many of their cities.

22

The Greeks were famous for their pottery, which they decorated with scenes from myths and from everyday life. The water jar on the left shows women at a fountain house. Above is a farming scene, with one man ploughing and another scattering seed. On the right is a soldier, or *hoplite*, in his armour.

explosion of the volcano on the nearby island of Thera may have had something to do with it. The palaces were abandoned except for Knossos, which was taken over by the Mycenaeans.

The Mycenaeans came from mainland Greece. They took over many Minoan ways of life and became the most important traders in the Mediterranean. But soon there came a very troubled time in the whole eastern Mediterranean. Cities were destroyed and pirates roamed the area. Even the art of writing was

A procession arrives at a Greek temple. Religion played an important part in the Greeks' lives. They had many gods and goddesses and told fascinating stories of their doings.

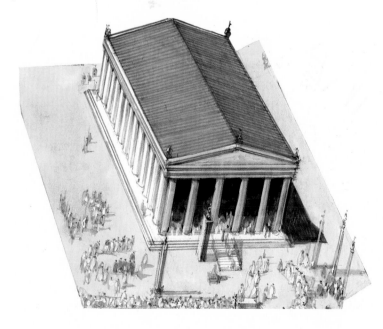

lost for a time. But gradually the region became more settled and new cities were founded.

City States Grow Up

By the 900s BC, there were little Greek cities on most of the Aegean islands, in Greece itself, and on the coasts of Anatolia. They were linked by having the same language and customs. As they grew rich they organized themselves into 'city states', made up of a main city, some villages, and the land around. Trading took place in the city's *agora*, or market place. At first people traded one sort of produce for another but in the 500s the Greeks began to pay for goods in coins. Greek goods, especially pottery and metal goods, were so beautiful that they were in demand in many other countries.

Each city had its own army and citizens were expected to fight for their city and to provide their own armour and weapons. The city of Athens, one of the most rich and powerful states, had a large, strong navy. When the Persians invaded (see page 24), the cities worked together to drive them out, but when the danger was over they fought one another again. But the Greeks were not just soldiers. Greek buildings and statues were so beautiful that people have admired them and tried to copy them ever since.

The Greeks were very interested in the world around them. They wanted to find out how and why people and the whole world of nature worked. Their careful studies were the beginnings of many modern sciences. The writings of their wise men on politics and on ruling well are still studied today.

Cyrus and Alexander

East of Mesopotamia, across the Zagros Mountains, lies the land that we now call Iran. It takes its name from nomads called Iranians, who moved into the area in about 1300 BC. Among the Iranians were two tribes called the Medes and the Persians, and they grew more powerful than the others. In the 500s BC King Cyrus II of the Persians, whose mother was a princess of the Medes, managed to gain control of the whole area. At once he set out to build up a great empire.

First Cyrus turned westwards, following the trade routes into Anatolia. He conquered the kingdom of Lydia, whose King Croesus was so wealthy that people still say 'as rich as Croesus'. One by one, Cyrus captured the Greek cities along the Anatolian coast. Then he turned south. He defeated the Babylonians and took over their empire (see page 15). He even planned to conquer Egypt, but he died before he could get there. His successors did overrun Egypt, and also conquered more land in the East as far as the river Indus.

Running the Empire

The Persian Empire was enormous. To make it easier to rule, the kings divided it into 20 provinces, each with a governor called a *satrap*, an army commander, and a tax collector. There were also inspectors known as the Ears of the King, who travelled around to make sure all officials were loyal to the king. Good roads were built to make it easier to travel throughout the Empire. Horses were kept at special rest houses, so the royal messengers could keep changing to fresh horses to speed up their journeys. The greatest road was the Royal Road, which stretched 2700 kilometres from Western Anatolia to Susa, the Persian capital. Messengers riding day and night could travel it in about nine days.

Soldiers of the Persian army were stationed in all parts of the Empire. They included archers, spearmen, and cavalry. Boys began military training when they were very young, and all men up to the age of 50 had to fight for their country if they were called on. The most important soldiers were the professionals, known as the Ten Thousand Immortals, a thousand of whom were chosen to make up the king's bodyguard.

Greek Invaders

The Greek cities of Anatolia were made part of the Persian Empire, but mainland Greece fought off the Persian invasions after terrible wars. Then the Greek cities went back to fighting one another. King Philip of Macedonia, to the north of Greece, forced them one by one to join him for a great expedition to invade the Persian Empire. He was killed in 336, before he could see his dream come true. His son Alexander was only 20 at the time and few people took him seriously. But he was a brilliant soldier who could plan both battles and sieges with equal skill. He was very brave and led his men into battle, riding Bucephalus, the great black horse he had trained himself. His men adored him.

Alexander crossed into Asia and in a few years had conquered the whole Persian Empire. He even

In the 500s BC King Darius of Persia began to build a great palace at Persepolis. His son Xerxes carried on the work, and when it was finished it was the finest of all the royal palaces. People now think that it may have been used for the New Year celebrations. There is a huge hall, where the king saw his people, with two great stairways leading up to it. On the stairways are carvings showing groups of people from all over the Empire, bringing their tribute to the king. The picture below shows a few of them. On the left is an Elamite, from southern Iran, carrying a lion cub. Next come a Babylonian with a banquet bowl, and a merchant from one of the Greek cities of Anatolia which Cyrus the Great conquered. The Bactrian camel, from the east of the Empire, may be led by a Parthian. The Scythian in front of him is carrying two metal armlets. He is wearing a sword. This may mean that the Scythians, who were nomads from north of the Black Sea, were allies of the Persians, and not their subjects. Last is an Indian, carrying a yoke in which are bags of gold dust. The Persians grew immensely rich on the tribute paid by their subjects from all over the Near East.

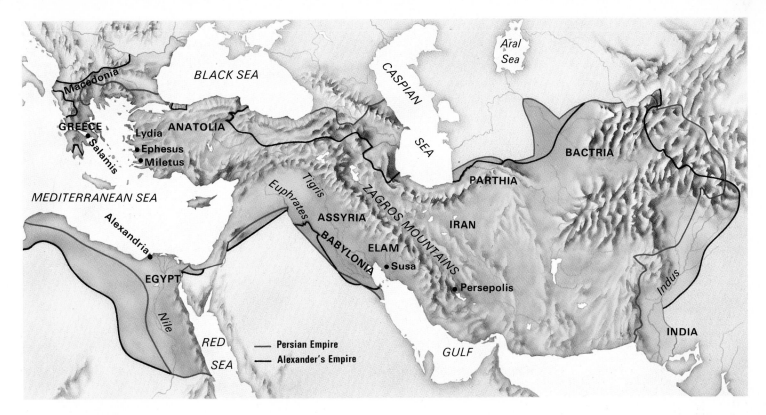

Left: This coin shows Alexander of Macedon, who is known as Alexander the Great. After he defeated the Persians he took control of their vast empire. The map above shows the area; the boundaries of the Persian Empire are shown in red, and those of Alexander's empire (which was slightly different) are in black.

After Alexander the Great died, his empire was divided up between his generals. But they and their families did not rule for very long. By the early centuries after the birth of Jesus, the lands along the Mediterranean were ruled by Rome, and those east of the Euphrates were controlled by members of an Iranian tribe called the Sassanians. They built great palaces where they lived in luxury. The walls were painted or covered with glass mosaics. The floors were set with mosaics or covered with silk carpets. This dish shows the Sassanian King Peroz I hunting ibexes. It is made of silver partly covered with a layer of gold. The Sassanians conquered an empire from the Mediterranean to Afghanistan, but in less than 20 years after they conquered Egypt, they themselves were defeated by the Muslim Arabs (see page 36)

invaded India. He was ready to go farther, but his men had had enough so he had to turn back. He hoped that the Greeks and Persians would become friends under his rule. He copied Persian customs and married a beautiful Persian called Roxane. But suddenly he died of fever. The generals who had served him so faithfully turned on one another. They murdered Roxane and her baby son and fought for power. At last they divided the Empire between themselves and became kings of Egypt, Asia, and Greece. India and parts of Asia broke away on their own.

Under these kingdoms, Greek styles, customs, and ideas were spread throughout the Near East. A form of the Greek language became the chief language of the Eastern Mediterranean countries. This is the language in which the New Testament was written. The great city of Alexandria, which Alexander founded in Egypt, became the largest and richest Greek city in the world and the home of many famous writers, thinkers, and scientists. The links of language and customs between the cities of the Near East lasted long after the kingdoms fell.

Travel and Trade

In ancient times, travel was a slow, difficult, and often dangerous undertaking. On land, almost everyone journeyed on foot. They walked along rough tracks, and merchants packed their goods on to the backs of donkeys. There were few roads in Europe before the Romans built them, while in China the roads were for the use of government officials. After about 1600 BC people began to use horses to ride and to draw chariots, and later camels to carry loads. Oxen pulled heavy carts, but these were very slow and got bogged down in the mud. Wherever it was possible, goods were carried by water.

Travel by Water

The Chinese built a network of canals which joined their main rivers. Goods and people travelled by boat all over the country. The Tigris and Euphrates in Mesopotamia, and the Nile in Egypt, were all busy waterways. The early Egyptians and Mesopotamians built boats out of the reeds that grew in the rivers. Boats were sometimes made of animal hides, and rafts were floated on blown-up animal skins. Sea-going craft were made of wood. The best timber came from the area of the east Mediterranean coast now called the Lebanon, where forests of great cedar trees grew. People from all over the Near East came to buy it.

Whenever possible, ships sailed within sight of land. If they had to cross open sea, they steered by the stars. Ships usually only sailed at times of year when they were likely to get good weather. The most famous sailors were the Greeks and Phoenicians.

Carthaginians beside their ship. Vessels like this were used for long sea journeys. In the 400s BC a Carthaginian called Hanno sailed from Carthage through the straits of Gibraltar, and then turned south down the coast of Africa. He may have sailed as far as Cameroon or Gabon. He describes rivers teaming with crocodiles and hippopotamuses, volcanoes, and even gorillas. The Carthaginians traded for gold with the Africans. Carthage might have become the greatest city of the Western Mediterranean, but it was wiped out by Rome after years of fighting.

They built ships with more than one bank of oars on each side, and sailed to the British Isles, India, and right round Africa, exploring and seeking trade.

Exchanging Goods

Even Stone Age hunters from different areas had met and exchanged goods. As time passed, the amount of trade between lands steadily increased. At first traders had to *barter*, exchanging goods that they agreed were of equal value. Then, by about 600 BC, coins began to be used in the country of Lydia in Anatolia. Soon people all over the Mediterranean area were using them. In China, too, people used coins (see page 20).

People usually wanted to exchange something they had plenty of, such as food or goods made by craftsmen, for some important necessity such as timber or metals which they lacked. If they had most of the things they needed in their own country, they could afford to buy luxuries like jewels and perfumes. Sometimes these came from far away. The blue stone called lapis lazuli was found only in Afghanistan, but it was traded all over the Near East. Cyprus takes its name from the copper found there, while Arabia produced resins like frankincense which gave off a fragrant smell when they were burned. Many of the countries round the Mediterranean, and the Greek colonies around the Black Sea coast, exported grain. Gold came from southern Egypt and silver, copper, and tin from Spain.

This Egyptian tomb-painting dates from about 1400 BC. It shows a heavily laden boat. Boats and ships were very important means of transport in the Ancient World, when there were few good roads. Travel by river or by sea was easier and cheaper than travel overland.

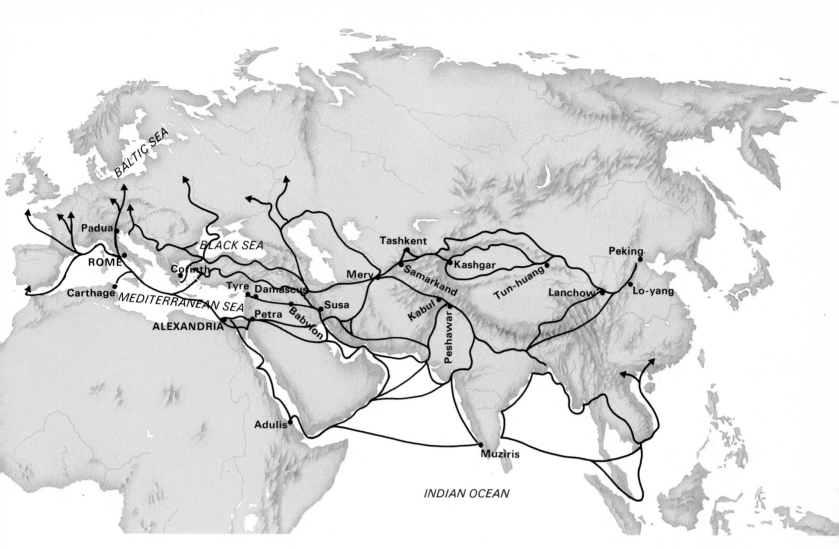

The map shows cities including: Padua, ROME, Carthage, Corinth, BALTIC SEA, BLACK SEA, MEDITERRANEAN SEA, Tyre, Damascus, ALEXANDRIA, Petra, Babylon, Susa, Mery, Samarkand, Tashkent, Kashgar, Tun-huang, Lanchow, Peking, Lo-yang, Kabul, Peshawar, Adulis, Muziris, INDIAN OCEAN

The Phoenicians

Some merchants did not just buy goods that their own people wanted. They also bought things to sell in other countries, acting as carriers. Both the Cretans and Mycenaeans may have traded in this way. Most successful of all were the Phoenicians. They lived on the coast of the Lebanon. Their three greatest cities were the ports of Byblos, Tyre, and Sidon. They were important traders in metals, searching out new supplies and then carrying them to customers all round the Mediterranean. At home their craftsmen were famous for their carved ivories and purple cloth, made with a dye obtained from shell fish. The Greeks too were great traders. Like the Phoenicians, they did not have enough land for all their people at home, and they set up colonies overseas. The Phoenician colony at Carthage on the north coast of Africa became so powerful that at one time it looked as if it might overcome Rome itself.

By the AD 100s there was a great deal of trade between Europe and Asia, much through Arab ships which sailed across the Indian Ocean, carrying glass and metals, cloth and pottery to exchange for silk, spices, and precious stones. Caravans travelled right across Central Asia, linking the great empires of Rome and China. But bandits made these overland routes dangerous.

The Romans built excellent roads, along which carts like the one below could travel. Most were pulled by oxen, which were strong but very slow. Horse collars had not yet been invented, which meant that horses pulling heavy loads would half strangle themselves if they went too fast. Horses were used to pull light chariots like the one at the top of this carving.

Rome and its Empire

The first great cities in Europe were built by the Greeks, in Greece itself and in Sicily, southern Italy, and even on the south coast of France. But gradually one of the cities of Italy grew powerful enough to conquer not only Greece but all the Mediterranean countries, and western Europe as far north as Britain. The empire of Rome was the largest, and the last, of the Ancient World.

According to one story, Rome was founded in 753 BC by twins called Romulus and Remus. They were said to be the sons of the war god, Mars. We do know for certain that farmers were settled in the hills by the river Tiber in the 700s BC. These first Romans led simple lives. There were a few traders and craftsmen, but most of them were farmers. At first kings ruled Rome, but they made themselves so unpopular that the Romans drove them out and set up a republic with an assembly for the citizens, a senate of nobles, and two consuls elected each year to lead them.

Building the Empire

At first Rome had to fight its neighbours to survive, and every male citizen was a soldier. The Romans were so successful that they conquered all Italy. The other nations round the Mediterranean became suspicious of Rome. They had to be defeated, and then the Romans had to fight more wars to protect what

This great arch stands among the ruins of Djemila, in Algeria. It was built by the Romans in AD 216. At this time Djemila was a thriving Roman town, on the same lines as others all over the Empire. North Africa was richer under the Romans than ever before or since. Today Djemila is a collection of ruins, half buried in the desert sands.

This Roman lamp shows a fisherman drawing in his nets. The Romans often decorated household objects with scenes of everyday life like this, from which we can build up a picture of the way they lived.

they had won. In a short time Rome built up a great empire. To do this, the Romans had to reorganize their army, turning it into a well trained force.

Sudden wealth and power caused much trouble among leading Romans. A terrible war broke out between rival politicians, during which the great general and dictator Julius Caesar was murdered. At last Caesar's great nephew defeated his rivals and set up a new kind of government with himself as Augustus, the first Emperor, leading it.

Life in the Empire

The Romans were very good at running their Empire. They spread their laws, taxes, and systems of government through the countries they ruled, and a Roman town in northern Europe was very like one in North Africa. It was built on the same pattern, and the people there wore Roman clothes and talked Latin, the Roman language.

When the Romans conquered north-west Europe, people known as the Celts were living there. Their chiefs and warriors lived in hill forts, while farmers grew grain and herded cattle, sheep and pigs on the land around. The Celts soon accepted Roman ways. The Romans built towns and cities, and a network of good roads to link them. Roman landowners brought new and better ways of farming, and cleared woodlands and drained marshes to provide more farmland. The frontiers were protected by a chain of walls and forts, to keep out barbarian raiders.

In North Africa, too, the Romans made many improvements. Thousands of kilometres of pipes took water to dry lands, so that farmers could grow grain, grapes, and olives, much of which was shipped back to Rome. North Africa became far richer than ever before or since.

In the eastern Mediterranean the Romans ruled over people whose ways of life were far older than their own. The Romans let them carry on much as before, and even copied many of their ways. The Romans particularly respected the learning and art of the Greeks. They copied many Greek sculptures and took a number back to Rome.

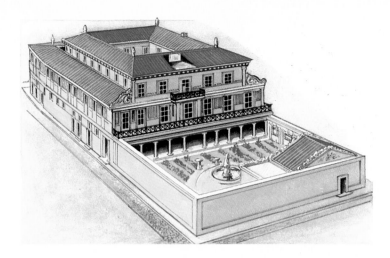

Left: A Roman villa in a town. It is built round a central courtyard, in which would be a pool and a fountain or perhaps some statues. There was also a garden. Rooms on the ground floor looked on to the courtyard or the garden. The rooms which gave on to the street were let out as shops.

The enormous size of the Roman Empire was its undoing. It was too vast for one man to rule over, and its borders were too long for the Roman armies to defend. The Roman Empire was officially divided into two: the Western Empire ruled from Rome, and the Eastern Empire ruled from Constantinople. Friendly barbarian tribes were brought into its armies to help in its defence. But this could not save it. Barbarian tribes invaded. The Eastern Empire managed to bribe them to go away, but the Empire in the west was overrun. The close links between the countries round the Mediterranean were broken for ever.

Right: A Roman soldier and his equipment. The soldiers complained that carrying so much made them no better than mules! Even so, Roman legions could march 48 kilometres (30 miles) a day, for many days at a time. They marched across the Empire, living in tents or in forts of stone or wood like the one below. Below: The Roman Empire at its greatest, in AD 117. At this time it was ruled by the Emperor Trajan, a Spanish general who reigned for 19 years. Before long, the Romans were driven out of Mesopotamia.

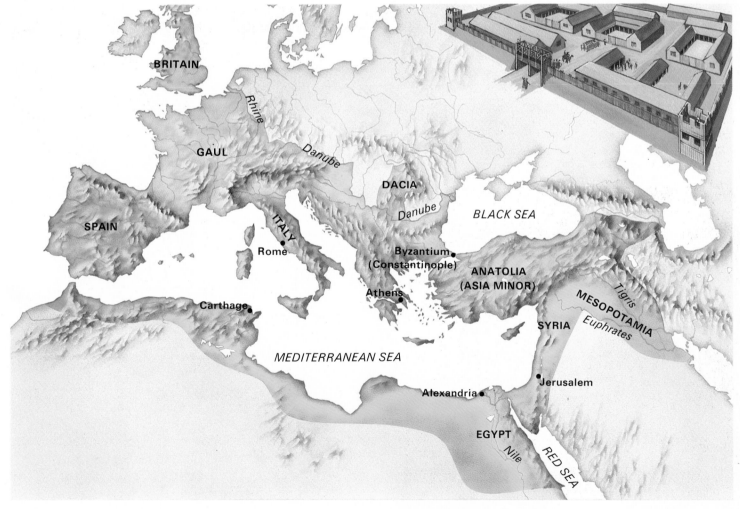

The Middle Ages

The great Roman Empire ruled the lands all round the Mediterranean Sea. It linked them with common laws and language. Traders sailed across the Mediterranean and travelled along the network of roads that spread all over the Empire. All this was changed when the barbarians overran the western half of the Roman Empire and its emperor gave up his throne in AD 476. The next thousand years are known as the Middle Ages, and during them the lands south and east of the Mediterranean developed in quite different ways from western Europe.

Byzantium and Islam

The eastern part of the Roman Empire was stronger and richer than the western part. It was able to pay the barbarians to move away. It became known as the Byzantine Empire, after its capital Byzantium, also known as Constantinople. Little more than 200 years after the fall of Rome, however, the Byzantine Empire faced a new and more dangerous threat than the barbarians. This was the growing Islamic Empire, which conquered more and more Byzantine lands.

The Byzantine Empire and the Islamic Empire were both cut off from northern Europe. Instead, they built up strong trading links with countries farther east. Muslim merchants sailed to India and on to the Spice Islands, and travelled overland as far as China. For a time, Europe became a backwater. Under the barbarians it was split into a patchwork of many small kingdoms. The old Roman roads became muddy tracks and robbers roamed the countryside. There was little travel or trade. In the 800s and 900s invaders from Scandinavia, called Vikings, raided and plundered the coasts. This time is sometimes known as the Dark Ages. Then, from the 1000s on, Europe began to grow more peaceful and its people became richer. But they now had little in common with the people of the Byzantine and Islamic countries.

The Holy Roman Empire

During the Middle Ages many of the little states in central Europe linked themselves in the Holy Roman Empire. Their rulers elected the strongest among them as emperor. The early emperors were crowned by the Pope, to show his approval, but later they did not bother with this. From the late 1300s the emperor always came from the Habsburg family which ruled Austria, the strongest state in the Empire. There were many quarrels between emperors and Popes; the emperors thought the Church should not tell rulers how to govern their countries, and the Popes thought emperors interfered in Church affairs.

IMPORTANT DATES	
481	Clovis became King of the Franks and soon built up a large kingdom in northern Europe.
570	Muhammad, the founder of the religion of Islam, was born in the trading city of Mecca in Arabia.
618	The T'ang Dynasty came to power in China.
622	The Prophet Muhammad fled from Mecca to the nearby city of Medina. This event is known as the Hjira and marks the first year of the Muslim calendar.
632	Muhammad died. Soon after his followers began to spread Islam all through the Near East.
711	The Moors (followers of Islam from Morocco) invaded Spain, and soon controlled most of Spain and Portugal.
771	Charlemagne became sole ruler of the Franks. He subdued the Saxons and converted them to Christianity, and fought the Moors in the Pyrenees. He helped the Pope defeat his enemies and in return was crowned 'Roman' emperor in 800.
787	The Vikings first invaded England. For the next two hundred years they menaced the coasts of northern Europe, burning and plundering towns and monasteries.
800	By now Ancient Ghana, south of the Sahara Desert in Africa, had become a major trading state. It was visited by many Arab merchants. Farther south, in modern Nigeria, the forest kingdom of Ife was growing up.
843	Charlemagne's empire was divided between his grandsons. Louis the German ruled east of the Rhine; Charles the Bald took France; and Italy, Provence, Burgundy, and Lorraine went to Lothair.
860	The Vikings discovered Iceland. Soon families from Norway were settling there as farmers. Norwegians and Danes also settled in eastern England and later in Normandy in France.
871	Alfred the Great became King of Wessex. He defeated the Danes and stopped them spreading into the west of England.
906	The Magyars, nomads from Central Asia who had settled in Hungary, began to invade Germany. Later they raided as far west as Italy and France before the German King Otto defeated them at the battle of Lech in 955 and they gave up westward raids.
962	The German King Otto, who wanted to revive the old Roman Empire, had himself crowned Emperor. He ruled over a collection of loosely linked German states, each with its own ruler. This became known as the 'Holy Roman Empire'.

Religion played a very important part in the daily lives of people in the Middle Ages. All over Europe they built the finest churches and cathedrals they could, for the greater glory of God.

986	The Vikings founded a colony in Greenland. In 1002 they reached North America.
1066	Duke William of Normandy invaded and conquered England. He is known as William the Conqueror.
1096	The First Crusade began after Pope Urban appealed to Christians to free the Bible Lands from the Muslim Turks.
1099	The Crusaders captured Jerusalem. The First Crusade was very successful and the Crusaders set up kingdoms in the lands they conquered. But the Muslims fought back and regained the area. Later Crusades could not win it back for the Christians.
1152	Eleanor of Aquitaine married Henry of Anjou. He later became King of England, so his and Eleanor's lands in France came under English rule. Henry took over Ireland in 1171. He was the first Plantagenet king of England.
1190	The Mongol leader Temujin began to build his empire. He became known as Genghis Khan. Peking was taken by the Mongols in 1215 and soon their empire reached westwards to the Gulf.
1215	The English Barons forced King John to agree to the Magna Carta, or Great Charter, stating their rights.
1240	The Mongols captured Moscow and destroyed Kiev. It looked as if they could not be stopped but the following year their Khan (ruler) died and they withdrew to Asia.
1271	Marco Polo set out with his father and uncle to visit the Mongol Emperor of China, Kublai Khan.
1337	The Hundred Years' War between England and France began. It was in fact a series of wars, lasting to 1453. The main cause was a claim by the kings of England to the throne of France. At first the English were very successful but in the end the French, inspired by the peasant girl Joan of Arc, drove the English from France.
1348	A terrible plague called the Black Death began to spread through Europe. Probably a third of the people there died from it.
1419	Prince Henry the Navigator sent his first expedition from Portugal down the western coast of Africa.
1434	Cosimo de' Medici became ruler of Florence. This Italian city was one of the greatest centres of the *Renaissance*, a new interest in art, learning, and science.
1440	At about this time two great empires were being built up in the Americas, those of the Incas in Peru and the Aztecs in Mexico.
1453	The end of the Hundred Years' War. In this year, too, the Turks captured Constantinople and the land round it, which was all that remained of the Byzantine Empire.

31

On the map (from left/top):

PICTS · IRISH · NORSE · SWEDES · FINNS · Volga · NORTH SEA · JUTES · ANGLES · BALTS · SLAVS · ANGLES · BRITISH · ANGLO-SAXONS · SAXONS · FRISIANS · SLAVS · London · English Channel · Rhine · THURINGIANS · BRETONS · Paris · ALAMANNI · RUGIANS · HUNS · ALANS · FRANKS · BURGUNDIANS · Lech · LOMBARDS · HUNS · BAY OF BISCAY · GEPIDS · GOTHS · SUEVI · BASQUES · OSTROGOTHS · BLACK SEA · VISIGOTHS · Danube · Rome · Constantinople (Byzantium) · EASTERN ROMAN EMPIRE · VANDALS · MEDITERRANEAN SEA · BERBERS

The Barbarians

When the Romans conquered Europe, they set the eastern boundaries of their Empire at the great rivers Rhine and Danube. In the forests and marshlands on the far side of these rivers lived tribes of people the Romans called barbarians. They made many raids across the frontier, looting Roman villas and towns.

In the AD 400s the barbarians were attacked from the east by the cruel and warlike Huns from Central Asia. The barbarians fled in front of them. They streamed across the frontiers and into the Roman Empire. There they set up their own kingdoms. Some tribes were very savage, and attacked the Roman towns. Rome itself was captured by barbarians, and in 476 the Roman emperor Romulus Augustulus had to give up his throne to a barbarian king. The Roman Empire in Western Europe had come to an end.

The Romans had built towns and cities all over Europe, linked by a network of good roads. People had travelled easily through all parts of the Empire, and had shared Roman laws and customs. Life under the barbarians was very different. They were farmers,

In the 400s barbarians from east of the Danube and Volga rivers flooded into the Roman Empire and settled there. The map above shows where the different tribes were living in 476, the year when the last emperor in the west gave up his throne. In the 400s and 500s the tribes shifted around. The Anglo-Saxons moved north and west across Britain, for example, while the Franks gained control of a large kingdom including much of modern France and Germany. The barbarians built villages of wooden houses, like the ones in the picture above.

and most of them kept clear of the stone-built Roman towns and cities. They lived in villages of wooden-framed houses, with walls of mud-plastered brush-wood and thatched roofs. Around the villages lay fields where they grazed cattle and sheep, while pigs rooted for food in the woods nearby. The barbarians grew a few crops, among them rye, wheat, and barley, and some peas and beans. Wool from the sheep was woven into cloth. Women wore long dresses and men short tunics over trousers. Warm cloaks of wool or fur were pinned on with jewelled brooches and clasps.

The barbarians were great fighters. The young men grouped together in warbands which raided and plundered. They thought the greatest virtues were courage and loyalty, and made up long poems telling of brave leaders and great battles. A man's most prized possession was his sword, which would often be a family heirloom.

In some parts of the old Empire little trace of the Romans was left. In England, which was invaded by Angles and Saxons, Roman ways of life disappeared altogether, to be replaced by those of the invaders. Only the roads and ruined buildings remained. But across the Channel many of the barbarians who settled among the Romanized people took up Roman customs. Their leaders thought of the Eastern Roman Emperor as their overlord. Even so, many Roman ways were replaced by barbarian ones. Roman skills were forgotten; there was no strong central government, and law and order broke down. Bands of robbers made it difficult to travel, and there was little trade over long distances. Europe changed from being part of one great empire into a patchwork of little kingdoms.

The Franks

One of the barbarian tribes to settle inside the Roman Empire was the Franks. They soon became more powerful than the tribes around them, and by 500 they ruled over a huge kingdom, including much of modern France and West Germany.

The greatest king of the Franks was Charlemagne, who came to the throne in 768. He spent all his reign in fighting. He brought the neighbouring countries under his control, and then fought against the heathen Saxon and Avars and Slavs in the east. He defeated them and made them become Christian. He helped the Pope defeat his enemies in Italy, and fought the Muslims on the borders of Spain. But Charlemagne also loved learning and education. He founded

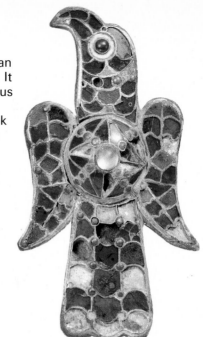

This brooch was made by an Ostrogoth in the late 400s. It is made of gold and precious stones. It shows an eagle, and was used to pin a cloak in position. The barbarians loved jewellery and were very skilled metal workers. They often showed animal forms.

schools and collected scholars around him at his court. He encouraged people to collect and copy books, and to spread Christianity. The Pope was so grateful to Charlemagne that he crowned him 'Roman Emperor'.

Vikings and Magyars

Two more great waves of invasion troubled western Europe in the early Middle Ages. In the late 700s, the people on the northern coasts were terrified by raiders from the sea. They came from Denmark, Sweden, and Norway, and we call them the Vikings. For the next 200 years, bands of up to 400 raiders would land on the beaches or sail up rivers, plundering towns and monasteries. Sometimes the Vikings were given huge sums of money to go away. But they were not all raiders. Some settled in Britain and France, and became farmers.

In the late 800s, about 25,000 Magyars moved from Central Asia to settle in the Hungarian Plains. From there, they rode west to raid Germany, Italy, and even France, plundering the country and terrifying the people. In 955 the Emperor Otto I defeated them at the battle of Lech. After this they settled down in Hungary and became farmers, and soon many became Christians.

The Vikings were great traders as well as raiders. They set up trading colonies at Novgorod and Kiev in Russia and farming and trading settlements in Greenland and Iceland. They reached America, where they traded for timber and furs.

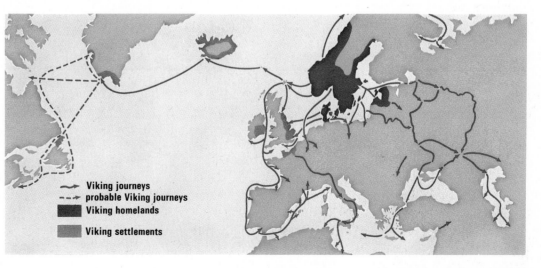

- → Viking journeys
- - -→ probable Viking journeys
- ■ Viking homelands
- ■ Viking settlements

The Spread of Christianity

Jesus Christ was born in the Roman province of Judea during the reign of King Herod the Great. This must have been in about 6 BC. For most of his life he lived in the village of Nazareth, but for three years he moved through the Holy Land, preaching and healing. His followers believed that he was the saviour God had promised them. After he was killed by the Romans in about AD 30, his followers began to teach other people to believe in him. Christian teachers travelled all through the Roman Empire, preaching their message and forming groups of Christians.

At first the Christians got into trouble because they refused to worship the Roman emperor as a god. Many of them were killed for their beliefs, and some of them were even eaten alive by lions to entertain huge crowds. But then, about 300 years after Jesus died, the Roman emperor himself became a Christian. Thousands of other Romans followed his example and Christianity became the official religion of the Empire.

There were many quarrels among the Christians. They disagreed about the way in which they should worship God, and even disagreed about exactly what they believed. The Christians in western Europe looked on the Bishop of Rome – the Pope – as their leader, while those in the eastern part of the Empire were led by the head of the Church in Constantinople. In the end the western and eastern Christians split into the Roman Catholic Church and the Eastern Orthodox Church.

When the barbarians overran western Europe in the 400s the organization of the Roman Empire broke

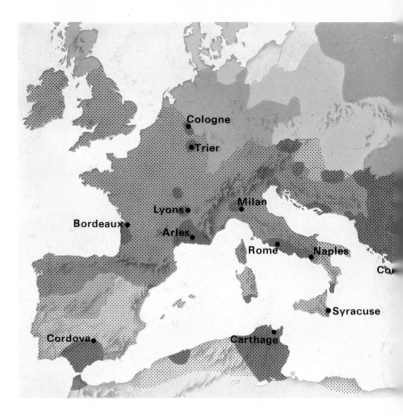

This map shows how Christianity spread through Europe and the Near East. The dotted area shows how far it had spread by 600. Much of this was later conquered by the Muslims. The Eastern Orthodox, or Byzantine, Church grew away from the Roman Church and split from it in 1054. Russia became Orthodox, but most of central Europe was converted by missionaries from the Roman Church.

down. As a result, the Christians became very important. Churchmen were often the only people who could read and write, and who had any experience of administration. Many took important places in government. The Church was the one strong link between the different barbarian kingdoms.

The Church had its own laws, and could fine people who disobeyed them. Its most severe punishment was *excommunication*. This meant cutting a person off from all the services of the Church. He could not be married or given Christian burial, and worst of all his sins would not be forgiven. If the Pope excommunicated a ruler, his subjects were no longer bound to be loyal to him. The Pope, as head of the Roman Church, became very powerful. His messengers travelled all over Europe and kept him in touch with everything that was happening. But as the Church became richer and more powerful, people began to resent its power, and the way it interfered in government. More and more people criticized the Church and its organization, until at last the Protestants broke away from the Roman Catholic Church in the early 1500s.

The Monasteries
Many Christians gathered together to live in monasteries and nunneries. At first they lived lives mainly of

This jewelled cross dates from about AD 1000. It comes from Constantinople. In the centre is the Virgin Mary, with Saint Basil and Saint Gregory on either side.

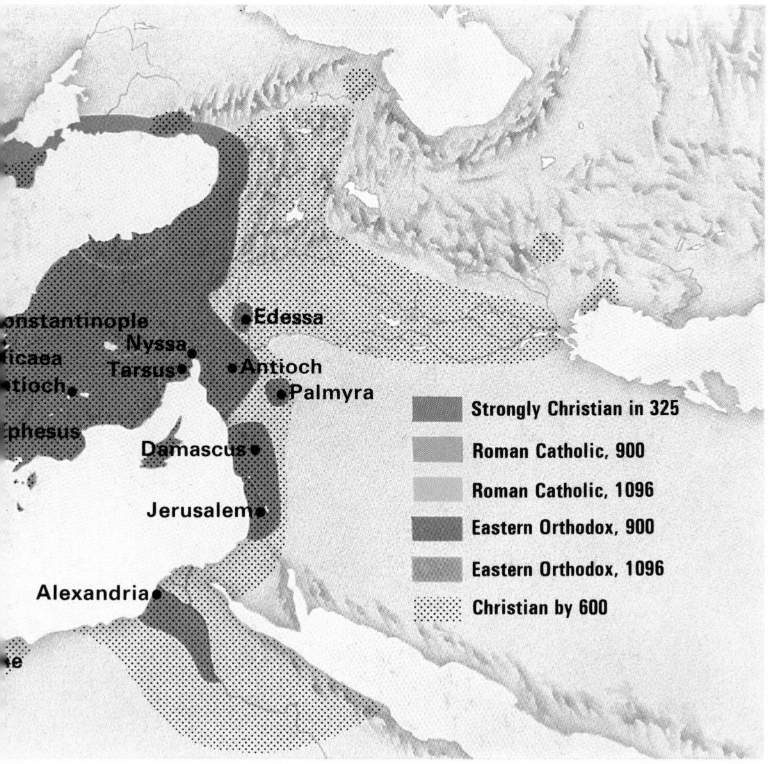
onstantinople
Nyssa
icaea
Tarsus
tioch
Edessa
Antioch
Palmyra
phesus
Damascus
Jerusalem
Alexandria
Strongly Christian in 325
Roman Catholic, 900
Roman Catholic, 1096
Eastern Orthodox, 900
Eastern Orthodox, 1096
Christian by 600

prayer. In the 500s St Benedict wrote down rules for his monks to live by. Much of their time was spent praying, but they also farmed the land to provide themselves with food. They reared fish in special ponds, and grew herbs for making their medicines. Many monasteries and nunneries kept bees, using the honey to sweeten their food and the wax for candles. Monks acted as doctors, caring for the sick and the poor, and travellers often stayed overnight in monasteries. In the libraries monks copied out books by hand. In the Middle Ages monasteries had almost the only libraries, and were centres of learning.

Other Christians who wanted to devote their lives to God became friars. They spent most of their time travelling through the country, preaching and teaching as they went.

The Missionaries

Christians have always believed in spreading their faith. The early Christians founded Churches all over the Roman Empire. Some of these were destroyed by barbarians, as was the Church in England; but before long missionaries from the Pope and from Ireland came over to teach people to become Christian again. Other missionaries were sent to the heathen people who lived east of the river Rhine. Many heathens were forced to become Christian by conquerors like Charlemagne, who killed all the people he overran who would not become Christian. In the 1200s the Teutonic Knights from Germany went to Poland to convert heathen Prussians. Meanwhile, the Eastern Orthodox form of Christianity was spreading northwards through eastern Europe, and to Russia. Even so, it was a long time before all Europe was Christian.

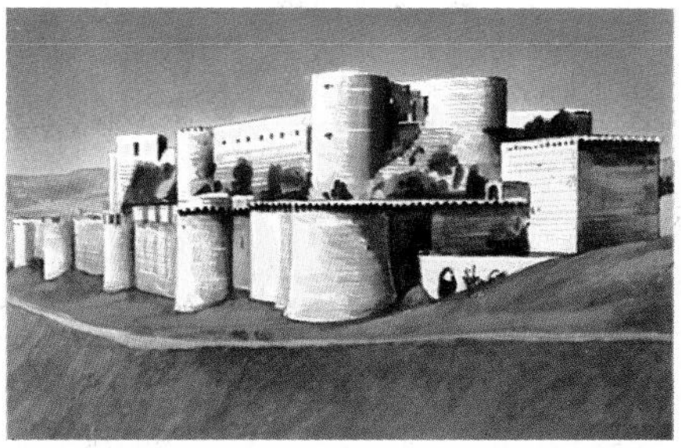

The castle of Krak des Chevaliers in Syria was built by the crusader Knights of St John, who helped and protected pilgrims. It withstood 12 sieges before it fell in 1271.

The Crusades

During the Middle Ages many Christians went on pilgrimages to visit holy places. These included great churches and places where saints were buried. The most important pilgrimage was the long journey to the Bible Lands. They believed that if they went on this pilgrimage their sins would be forgiven. In the 1000s the Bible Lands were conquered by the Muslim Turks. They robbed, tortured, and even killed many pilgrims. At last the Pope called for a holy war or Crusade against the Turks. Soldiers from all over Europe gathered at Constantinople, and then attacked the Bible Lands. Soon they had captured Jerusalem and driven the Turks from most of the area.

The First Crusade was a great success, but soon the Turks fought back. Several more crusades were called, but without success. Many of the crusaders quarrelled among themselves and several expeditions never even reached the Bible Lands. King Richard the Lionheart of England, one of the greatest and most successful of all crusaders, came within sight of Jerusalem but even he could not recapture it. In the end, the Christians had to admit defeat.

This stained glass was made in Germany in the 1400s. It shows St Bernard reaping in the fields. St Bernard was the abbot of Clairvaux in France in the 1100s, and was responsible for founding many other monasteries. The monks who lived there spent part of their time praying, and the rest working in the fields, the library, and the workshops which formed part of the community.

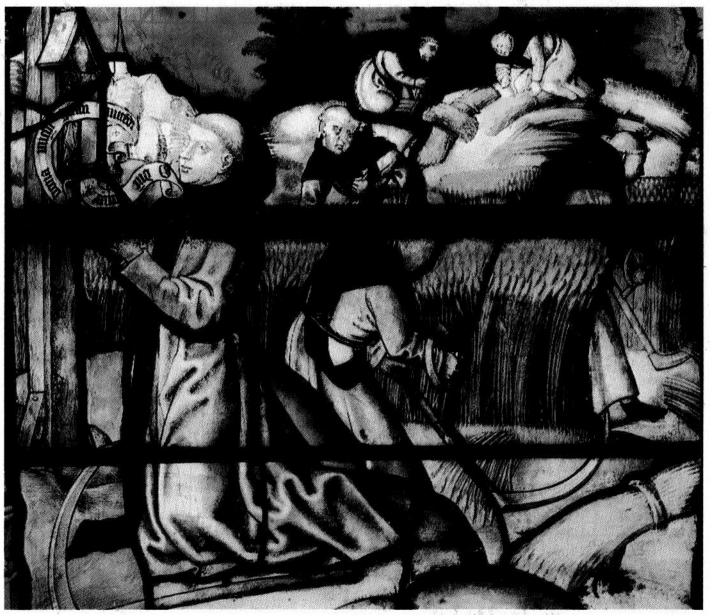

The Rise of Islam

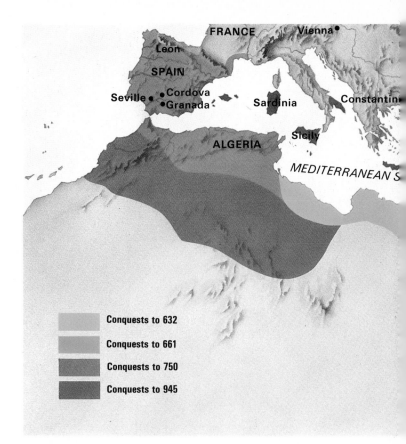

Conquests to 632

Conquests to 661

Conquests to 750

Conquests to 945

In the 600s a great new religion began. It is called *Islam*, which means 'Submission to the Will of Allah' (God), and the people who believe in it are called Muslims. In less than a hundred years the Muslims spread out from the town of Mecca in Arabia to rule an empire that stretched from Spain in the west, eastwards to the borders of India.

The religion of Islam was founded by the Prophet Muhammad. Muslims believe that the angel Gabriel appeared to Muhammad and told him Allah's commands and teachings, which he passed on to his companions. Later they were collected into a single book, the *Koran*, which is the holy book of the Muslims. Muslims share many beliefs with Jews and Christians, and honour the great Jewish prophets. They respect Christ as a great prophet, but do not believe that he is God.

At first few people believed Muhammed's teachings, but before he died he had gained many followers. They wanted to spread their faith as widely as possible. Muslim warriors on camels and horses moved north and east, overrunning the neighbouring lands. Often they were welcomed by the people who lived there, who had suffered under the harsh rule of the Byzantine and Persian empires. Muslim rule spread amazingly quickly, and with it spread the language of Arabic, in which the *Koran* was written.

This painting shows the Prophet Muhammad with his followers before the battle of Uhad. There was no water, and in a miracle water streamed from the Prophet's fingers. Muslim artists are forbidden to show Muhammad's face, so it has been veiled.

Life under the Muslims

The Muslims borrowed and improved on the best ideas of the peoples they conquered. They translated the works of the Ancient Greeks into Arabic, and learnt what they had known of medicine, mathematics, astronomy, and mechanics. The Arab scientists became the best in the world. The Arabs had a great respect for learning and under them many people learnt to read and write. Their traders learnt how to make paper from the Chinese, and learnt how to write down numbers with nine digits and a nought, as we do today, from the Indians.

All over the Muslim empire people lived in the same sort of way, for the teachings of Islam laid down many rules for everyday life. People could travel safely from one end of the great empire to the other, so trading became safe and easy. The spread of the Arabic language meant that merchants from different countries could understand one another, and a single kind of gold coin, the dinar, was used all through the empire. Much of the Muslim gold came from Africa, in return for salt. Muslim traders carried their goods on camels, donkeys, or mules, roped together in processions called caravans. Most of the trade was in luxuries: glass and silk from Syria, gold and ivory from Africa, furs from north of the Black Sea, and spices from the Far East. Wood was brought from Europe, for ship-building, heating the glass kilns, and for lining water channels. The Muslims were very good farmers. They set up vast schemes for watering the land so that crops could be grown. In Spain, for example, they could grow sugar cane, rice, and cotton.

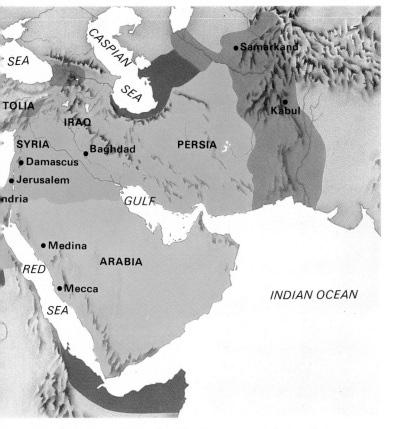

This map shows how the Muslims spread their religion through the southern Mediterranean and Near East, building up a vast empire in an amazingly short time.

The Rise of the Turks

For the first few years the Muslim lands were ruled by a single *caliph*. But then many provinces broke away to be ruled by their own *sultans*. The most important of these were Turks. The Turks were nomads from Central Asia, who first came into the Islamic world as slaves. Then they became Muslims, and became the Empire's most important soldiers. They soon gained control of much of the Near East, and then moved north to the Byzantine Empire. They moved into Anatolia, which is now called Turkey after them. They settled down and built up a prosperous state there. The most important branch of the Turks was the Ottomans. Bit by bit they won control of the old Byzantine Empire, first conquering the Balkan countries, and then almost all Anatolia, until only the Byzantine capital, Constantinople, and a little land round it remained. In 1453 the Turks captured even this last stronghold.

Soon the Ottomans ruled over a Muslim empire from Algeria to Iraq. They controlled much of the Mediterranean shipping, and several times invaded Europe, even threatening the Holy Roman Empire's capital, Vienna. They kept their empire together by an extraordinarily efficient system of government, with officials in every village. But above all, it was held together by the Muslim faith.

This picture was painted in Baghdad in 1237. It shows a trader about to mount his camel and set off on an expedition. Merchants travelled all over the Islamic empire, carrying their goods on donkeys, camels, and mules roped together in processions called caravans. Arab merchants also controlled the trade from the East to Europe, which passed through Muslim lands.

Feudal Life

In the early Middle Ages, kings and chiefs did not have enough money or plunder with which to reward the men who fought for them. Instead, they rewarded them by giving them land. Out of this grew up what we call the feudal system, because land given like this was called by the Latin word *feudum*.

Under the feudal system each state was ruled by a king or prince. He owned all the land, but gave large areas of it to his nobles. In return they promised that they and their men would fight for him when needed, be loyal, and carry out certain other duties. Kings and nobles lived in large stone castles that were usually cold and uncomfortable. From their castles nobles ruled the surrounding countryside. In war, the people who lived nearby brought their flocks and herds inside the castle walls to take shelter from the enemy.

The great nobles were bound to raise an army for their king. It was made up of mounted knights in heavy armour, carrying swords and lances, and foot soldiers armed with bows and pikes. A noble's son served first as a page and then as a squire before taking his oath of loyalty to his lord as a knight.

Nobles divided up their large estates into smaller units called manors, which they gave to knights on roughly the same terms as those between the noble and the king. On every manor there were peasants who worked the land. A lucky few held their land freely, without conditions, but most were *villeins*. They had to work in their lord's fields for two or three days a week. They could not marry or leave the manor without his permission, and they had to pay certain dues.

Life on the Land

Round their small, draughty huts, peasants had plots of land where they could grow vegetables. But most of the village land was divided into three large fields. Each man held several strips of land, scattered across each field. It was usual to grow wheat in one field, and barley in the second, and leave the third fallow (unsown) so it could get back its goodness. Each year the crops were changed round and a different field was fallow.

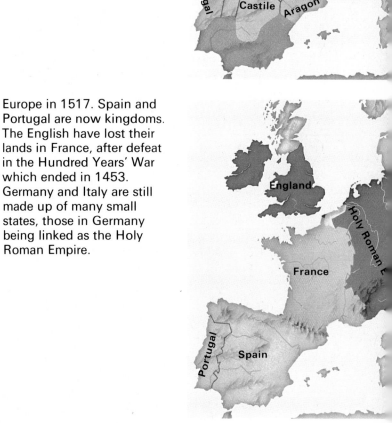

Europe in 1173. At this time the king of England ruled over more of France than the French king! Some of these lands had belonged to Duke William of Normandy, who conquered England in 1066. The rest had come through marriages. Spain was mostly ruled by Muslims, known as Moors.

Europe in 1517. Spain and Portugal are now kingdoms. The English have lost their lands in France, after defeat in the Hundred Years' War which ended in 1453. Germany and Italy are still made up of many small states, those in Germany being linked as the Holy Roman Empire.

A castle under siege in the Middle Ages. In times of war peasants from the country round a castle would come with their animals to shelter inside its walls. Attackers surrounded the castle and tried to break into it. They battered the walls with huge rams, and hurled stones at them with catapults. They wheeled siege towers against the walls from which they could jump up to the ramparts. They camped round the castle and hoped to starve out the people inside. The defenders shot at them with arrows, and dropped stones and boiling oil on them.

This picture was painted in the 1400s. It shows peasants at work on the land outside the great castle of Lusignan in western France. A peasant is ploughing with a pair of oxen. Others are tending their vines and herding sheep. The picture comes from a 'Book of Hours' painted for the duke of Berry, the brother of the king of France, who was a great landowner. The book contained a calendar of the months with saints' days, then psalms, litanies, and prayers, illustrated with scenes from the lives of Jesus and Mary. The calendar has one painting for each month, showing its activities. This picture shows the month of March.

Each village had a large common where everyone was allowed to graze their sheep and cattle. They could feed their pigs and collect wood in the forests, but they were not allowed to hunt the game. That belonged to the lord. There was never enough hay to feed all the animals through the winter. Each autumn many of them were killed off and their meat was salted to provide food during the winter.

It was a tough, hard life and people often went hungry. They knew nothing of germs and the spreading of diseases and very little about treating illness. In 1348 a terrible new disease spread to Europe from the East. It was far worse than anything people had ever known. This was the Black Death.

This terrible plague is thought to have killed one person in every three, right across Europe. Whole villages were wiped out.

In the early days the feudal system worked quite well, particularly in France and England. One problem was that great landowners could become more powerful than their king. They often rebelled. And after the Black Death there were fewer peasants to work the land. Those that were left wanted more freedom and better conditions. All over Europe peasants revolted against their masters, and in many countries feudal society was brought to an end. In central and eastern Europe, however, the feudal way of life lasted well into the 1800s.

39

The Mongol Empire

In the early 1200s a number of wandering tribes who lived in Central Asia joined together under an amazing leader. They called him Genghis Khan, which meant 'the very mighty lord'. Under him and his family these Mongol tribes conquered a vast empire, which stretched from China in the east to Hungary in the west.

The Mongols came from the steppes of Mongolia. Here there are wide, flat, treeless plains, overlooked by high, snow-topped mountains. Winter is bitterly cold, and in summer the burning sun turns the soil to dust while plants wither and die in the heat. The Mongols lived a *nomadic* life, moving around with their flocks and herds in search of grazing. They lived in round felt tents which could be packed on to ox carts, while men and women travelled on stocky, bad-tempered ponies.

The Mongol Army

The Mongols spent a great deal of time fighting. Often the different tribes fought one another, but Genghis Khan made them into a huge, organized army. Soldiers on the move rode in small groups of about ten men, carrying with them their basic rations of smoked mutton and dried milk. Each man had five ponies, ridden in turn so that they would not get tired. The Mongols guided their tough and speedy ponies with their feet, so that their hands were free to shoot arrows and throw javelins. They travelled at great speed, covering hundreds of kilometres in a day. Messengers rode from one group of men to another, and at night they used drums, horns, shouts, and even bird calls to signal to one another.

Empire Builders

Genghis Khan led his Mongol hordes (troops) first into China and then westwards across Central Asia. He soon learnt how to besiege cities that held out against him, and break down their walls. A few craftsmen who would be useful were taken prisoner, but most people were killed and their heads cut off. The land around was laid waste, and it was often years before anything could grow there.

People were so terrified of the Mongols that they often surrendered without fighting. Genghis Khan did not harm them or their cities. Once the Mongols had conquered an area they were good rulers. The

Left: Genghis Khan, the greatest of all Mongol leaders.
Right: The Mongol Empire stretched from China right into Europe. The Mongol armies travelled very quickly and usually took their enemies by surprise. The cities on the map are cities burned down by the Mongols, and the arrows show their main invasion routes.

Yasak, as the Mongol laws were called, was obeyed all through the empire. The Khan paid informers to tell him what was happening in distant places, and messengers called arrow riders carried his orders for 400 kilometres a day on relays of ponies. Trade went on busily, and travellers, merchants, and even missionaries made journeys safely back and forth across Asia.

The Mongol empire was too huge for one man to rule. In the late 1200s it was divided into four Khanates. But the Khans quarrelled among themselves and the people they ruled over grew strong enough to drive them out. A Mongol called Babur built up a new empire in India in the 1500s, but most of the Mongols went back to the steppes and took up their old nomadic way of life once more.

The Mongols in Europe

In the 1240s the Mongol hordes poured through south Russia, Poland, and Hungary. They burned down cities, killed thousands of people, and laid waste the countryside. They easily defeated the slow-moving European soldiers sent against them. It seemed that only a miracle could stop them. Suddenly, they packed their tents and turned eastwards. Their Great Khan Ogadei had died, and they had been called back to vote for a new Khan. South Russia was ruled by them for more than a hundred years to come, but the rest of Europe had been saved.

A Mongol camp today. Now, as hundreds of years ago, the Mongols live in felt tents called *yurts*. They move around looking for grazing for their flocks and herds.

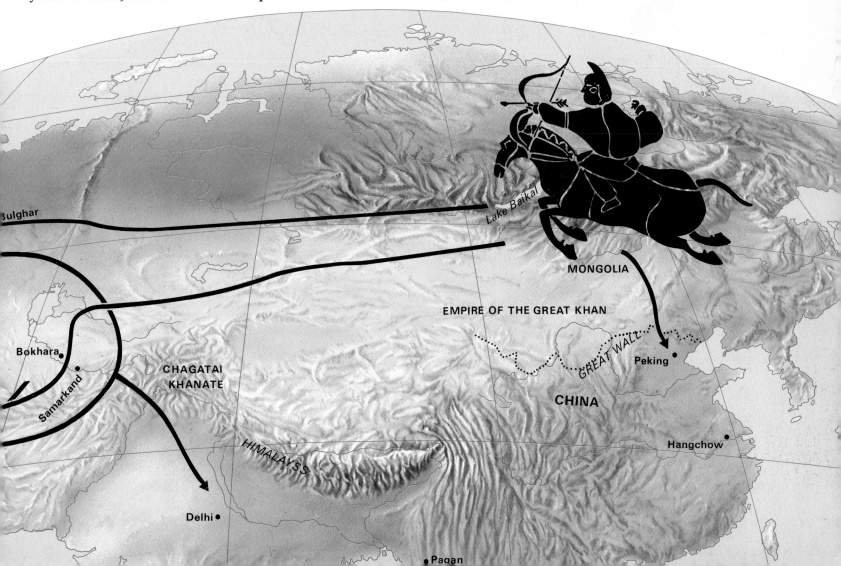

Travel and Trade

When western Europe was overrun by the barbarians, it became cut off from the Mediterranean countries and their trade. In the Eastern Roman Empire and the Muslim countries, trade grew busier than ever, and more and more of it was with the East. Arab merchants travelled right across Central Asia along routes like the Silk Road, which led from the Black Sea to China. Here they bought silk, porcelain, salt, and spices in return for gold and jade. Other Arabs went by sea to India and then eastwards to the Spice Islands (see page 49).

Meanwhile trade in western Europe had slowed to a trickle. The Roman roads were not repaired, and soon they became muddy tracks. What trade there was went mostly by sea or river. Each village produced most of the things its people needed, such as food, clothes, and tools. There were regular markets, where people could meet and exchange goods made locally. But some necessary things, such as salt, could often

A group of merchants following the camels on which their goods are laden. This painting comes from a map of Central Asia and China made in about 1375. Its information came largely from the writings of Marco Polo.

not be found locally. And by the 1000s people were becoming richer. They wanted luxuries such as sugar, spices, wine, and silks that came from abroad. To get such things, they had to visit a large town or city.

Town Life

Medieval towns and cities in Europe were very small by our standards. Some grew up around Church centres, but many began as trading settlements, at good harbours along the coasts or inland where trade routes crossed. Others were founded by kings or nobles, who promised good conditions to attract people. For the townspeople were outside the feudal system. People in the towns worked as traders or craftsmen. Each craft was governed by a guild, which saw that its members produced goods of a high standard. It set prices and wages, and punished cheats. A boy who wanted to join a guild had to work for several years as an apprentice to a master.

Travel was difficult and dangerous. The trade routes followed the old Roman roads, even though they were now just mud and gravel. Along them went

This pottery group of a bullock cart and traders was made in China during the T'ang Dynasty, which lasted from the 600s to the 900s. The faces and clothes of the traders show that they were not Chinese. Thousands of foreign merchants lived in China, or travelled there across the mountains and deserts of Central Asia.

Princess Isabella of France goes to meet her husband, King Richard II of England, in 1396. She travels in a splendid litter, supported by horses.

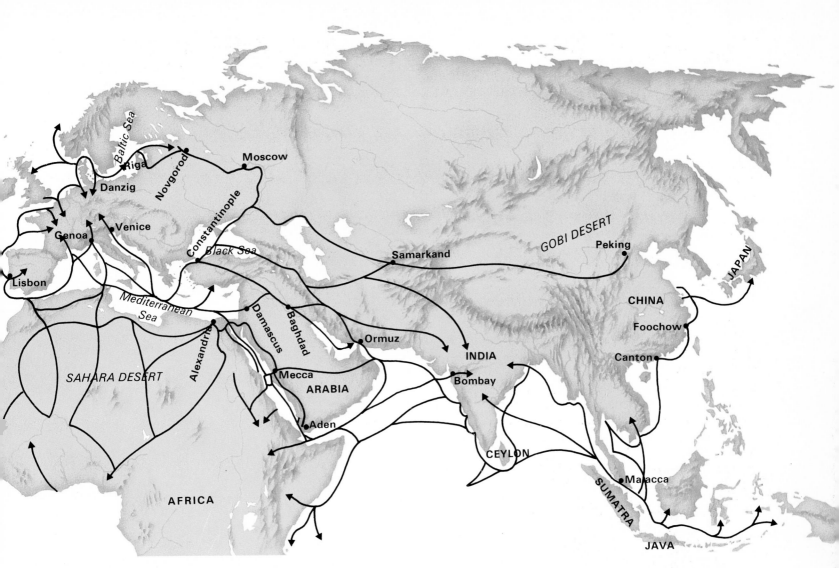

soldiers, pilgrims visiting a holy shrine, stonemasons seeking work, and merchants trading. Rich people travelled on horses, but most people walked. Merchants loaded their goods on to pack horses, for heavy carts often overturned or got stuck. Bandits lurked on lonely stretches of road, and no one dared travel after dark. Where two main trade routes crossed, fairs grew up. In the Champagne region of France, for example, where roads from Italy, southern France, Flanders, and Germany crossed, huge fairs lasting as long as six weeks were held each year.

From the north of Europe and the countries round the Baltic Sea came grain and furs, flax and herrings, copper and iron. England was specially famous for its wool, much of which was woven into cloth in Flanders. A great deal of the northern trade was carried out by merchants from towns which banded together in the Hanseatic League, protecting one another's merchants and helping to keep roads safe. From southern Europe came wine and olives. For many years the Italians had almost complete control of the trade with the East, and in particular the spice trade. Everyone else had to deal through them, and pay whatever prices they chose to charge. Gradually other European merchants became bolder and began to travel farther and farther to the East.

A market place in the 1400s. People from the countryside around would bring their goods to the local market town, where they would sell them and buy what they could not produce themselves. Round the market place were streets of small shops, with symbols hanging outside to show what they sold; a cobbler would hang out a shoe, for example. People selling the same thing, or working in the same trade, often had shops next to one another. People who lived in towns were outside the feudal system. They owed allegiance to the king, or to the noble who had founded the town.

43

Early America

In about 26,000 BC bands of hunters crossed the ice between the easternmost point of Asia and the western tip of America. But soon this ice bridge melted, and the people of America were cut off from the rest of the world. In about 1000 some Vikings landed on the north-east coast, and for a time traded there. But until Christopher Columbus arrived in 1492, the Americans developed in a way which had nothing to do with Europe.

The people of North America were mostly hunters, adding to their food supply by gathering roots, berries, and nuts. They built tents and shelters out of skins and branches, tied together with thongs of animal hide. Some, like the Iroquois, who lived in the north-eastern woodlands, became farmers, growing beans, maize, and squash (a sort of marrow). They built their wooden houses inside a palisade of wooden stakes which protected them from attack. Farther south, the Pueblo Indian farmers built mud brick buildings like great blocks of flats. These had several hundred rooms built round a central courtyard, which were entered by holes in the roofs.

The American Empires
In Central and South America, in what are now Mexico and Peru, great empires grew up where people lived in cities as fine as many in Europe and the

This stone slab was carved by the Mayas of Central America. They were a farming people who built no real cities, but they did build great religious centres with tall pyramid temples and palaces. The Mayas were important from about 1000 BC to about AD 900, when they abandoned palaces and villages. No one knows why. This carving of about AD 709 shows a priest carrying a staff. Before him kneels a guilty man, who is hurting his own tongue with a rope of thorns.

East. The Incas, who lived around Cuzco in the Andes, first began to grow powerful around AD 1200, but they did not conquer their enormous empire until the 1400s. The Aztecs, too, only controlled Mexico from the late 1400s. Both had their own customs, but their way of life was based on that of the earlier people of the area.

There are three distinct areas in Peru, each with its own climate. On the coast is a desert strip broken by fertile valleys, where rivers flow down to the sea. Then come the high Andes Mountains, and behind them are great tropical rainforests. Mexico too is a mixture of highlands and lowlands, deserts and tropical forests.

Wheat and barley were unknown to the Americans. They grew maize and the many local vegetables. In the Andes, the hardy potato was the main crop in places where the climate was harsh. There were none of the Old World farm animals, and no horses. The Incas of Peru kept guinea pigs and some ducks for meat, and the Aztecs of Mexico had turkeys and small hairless dogs. Hunting, trapping, and fishing added to the larder, and the Incas tamed llamas and used them to carry loads. Ordinary houses were built of *adobe*, sun-dried mud bricks, or of stone. Great fortresses and monuments were made of stone.

None of the peoples of Mexico and Peru used the wheel, although little wheeled toys have been found there. The country they lived in was not suitable for wheeled vehicles, and llamas could not have pulled carts. Iron was unknown, and many of their tools and weapons were made of stone. Some were made of copper, and their skilled craftsmen used copper, gold, and silver to make splendid jewellery, figures, and vessels.

The Inca emperor was called *The* Inca, and he claimed to be descended from the Sun God. Everyone in his empire had their own special place in society, according to the work they did. The state made sure that people would be fed and cared for, even in times of misfortune, provided they did their work and were

The Aztecs wrote records and histories in a kind of book which we call a *codex*. It was made of a single strip of limewashed leather, which was then folded up. The Aztecs wrote in glyphs – pictures which represent words. This picture shows part of a codex.

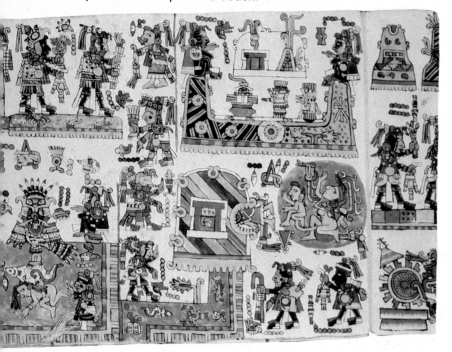

Two of the many different North American shelters: a bark tepee built by Cree Indians, and a Creek Indian house of branches.

An Aztec stone carving.

good citizens. The Incas did not have a form of writing. Instead, they used *quipus* to keep records. A quipu was made up of a main string, with other coloured strings tied on to it. Colours and knots represented goods and numbers. The Incas built roads to cross their great empire, with relays of runners to carry news. In the mountains, suspension bridges made of plaited reeds crossed ravines. Canals carried water to fields in the valleys, while in the Andes, where good land was scarce, terraces were cut up the mountain slopes to make flat land for growing crops. Llamas, alpacas, and vicunas grazed in the mountains. The Inca women were expert weavers and wove their wool into fine cloth to wear in the cold regions. Cotton clothes were worn in hot places.

An Inca gold figure.

The Aztec capital, Tenochtitlan, was built on the marshy islands of a lake. Mud from the lake was used to join the islands together and to make floating gardens where vegetables were grown. The emperor had a splendid palace and there were temples to the many gods. The Aztecs believed that life would vanish from the Earth unless the gods were kept strong. So they offered the most precious sacrifice of all: the blood of human hearts. Thousands of victims were sometimes killed in one ceremony. The Aztecs often went to war to capture victims for sacrifice. The people they conquered also had to send them tribute, including gold, silver, jade, turquoises, parrot feathers, and maize.

An earthenware vase made by the Mochica people of Peru.

The Age of Discovery

In the 1450s people in Europe and Asia did not know that the Americas and Australia existed. They did not even know that it was possible to sail south round the tip of Africa. But soon all this changed. Sailors from Portugal sailed round Africa into the Indian Ocean in 1488, and ten years later reached India itself. In 1519 another Portuguese expedition set out to make the first voyage around the world.

These early explorers were very brave. When they set out into unknown seas many people told them they would find whirlpools and boiling seas, strange monsters, and flames rising from the water. Some people thought the Earth was flat, and that the explorers would sail over the edge of the world into nothing! Conditions on board their sturdy little ships were often terrible. Sometimes they were months without sighting land, and their food and water supplies went bad and even ran out. But their voyages and discoveries changed the lives of everyone in Europe. They opened a new way to the Spice Islands of the Far East, and found a whole new world in the Americas.

The explorers were not the only people to make discoveries at this time. Back in Europe, people were discovering again the knowledge of the Ancient Greeks and Romans. Much of this had been lost since the barbarians took over the Roman Empire a thousand years earlier, but now wealthy people were paying scholars large sums to collect libraries of old books. In the 1450s printing was invented, which meant that books could be made quickly and cheaply. Many copies of new and old books were printed.

More and more people learnt to read and they began to think and ask questions about everything they were taught. Until then people had thought that the Earth was the centre of the Universe, and that the Sun, planets, and stars moved round it. Now scientists began to study the movements of all the objects in the sky. They discovered that the old ideas were quite wrong and that the Earth moved round the Sun. Other people began to look at the way in which their bodies worked. They found out how blood moves round the body, and how the bones and muscles are arranged.

Looking for new ideas could be as dangerous as looking for new countries. Many people did not want to have the old ideas questioned, so scientists were sometimes punished severely for their new ideas. Some of them were even tortured. But nothing could stop them from making their discoveries, or stop the new ideas from spreading.

A New Church

In the 1400s people began to question the teachings of the Church. At this time Bibles were written in Greek or Latin, which ordinary people could not understand. They only knew what the priests told them. Some people thought that the Bible ought to be translated into ordinary languages like English and German, so that people could find out for themselves what it said. At the same time, many people disliked the way the Church was run. In 1520 a group of Christians split away from the Catholic Church and set up their own organization. They were known as Protestants, and soon millions of people joined them. For the next two hundred years there were terrible quarrels between Catholics and Protestants which sometimes broke out into wars.

IMPORTANT DATES

1450s Printing was invented in Germany. This meant that books could be made cheaply and quickly. New ideas could spread rapidly. Soon many more people learnt to read.

1453 The Ottoman Turks captured the Christian city of Constantinople. They soon ruled over Turkey, North Africa, Egypt, Arabia, and south-east Europe.

1485 Henry VII became King of England. He was the first Tudor king. He, his son Henry VIII and his granddaughter Queen Elizabeth all helped to make England great.

1488 Bartolomeu Dias sailed round the southern tip of Africa into the Indian Ocean. Soon many other sailors voyaged into the Indian Ocean and on to the Spice Islands.

1492 Christopher Columbus sailed across the Atlantic Ocean and reached the West Indies. Later he went on to the coast of Central America.

1497 John Cabot discovered Newfoundland, a huge island off the coast of Canada, for Britain.

1517 The Protestant Christians began to break away from the Roman Catholic Church. Protestants and Catholics later fought many terrible wars against each other.

1519 The first ships to sail round the world set out from Europe under Ferdinand Magellan.

1547 Ivan IV became Tsar (ruler) of Russia. For a long time Russia had been ruled by Mongols but Ivan, who was known as 'the Terrible', drove them out. He encouraged Russian explorers to travel east and explore Siberia.

1608 The telescope was invented. One of the first people to use it was the Italian scientist Galileo. He was imprisoned for saying that the Earth was not the centre of the Universe.

1630 The Japanese stopped Europeans entering their country. The Japanese and the Chinese both had powerful kingdoms and neither wanted anything to do with Europeans for several hundred years.

1643 Louis XIV became king of France, at the age of five. When he grew up he believed that a king should do whatever he wanted, and he organized France so that he could have his way. In the 1600s and 1700s France, Spain, and Austria

Christopher Columbus sets out to sail westwards across the Atlantic. He took three ships, the *Santa Maria*, the *Nina*, and the *Pinta*. He believed that he could sail round the world to the East Indies, and did not know that America lay in between. After more than a month at sea he sighted land. He had found the West Indies. He thought that they were islands off the coast of China! He made three more journeys across the Atlantic and explored several islands and part of the mainland coast of America. But to the end of his life he believed that he had reached Asia.

were all very powerful countries. They fought each other several times but none of them ever got control of the others.

1682 Peter the Great became Tsar of Russia. He wanted to make Russia a great and powerful country. He travelled through Europe, learning how the western countries did things. When he got back to Russia he taught his people western ways.

1750s The British East India Company won control of India from the French.

1759 The British gained Canada from the French.

1769 Captain James Cook set out to explore the Pacific. He claimed New Zealand and eastern Australia for Britain.

The Great Explorers

For most of the Middle Ages, Europe was cut off from the rest of the world. Trade in silks, spices, and jewels from Asia was in the hands of Arab merchants, who travelled overland or sailed the Indian Ocean to China and the Spice Islands in their speedy wooden dhows. They brought their cargoes back to the Mediterranean, where they sold them to Europeans at an enormous profit.

Towards the end of the Middle Ages, European merchants began to travel farther and farther east. In the late 1200s Niccolo, Maffeo, and Marco Polo journeyed overland to Peking in China. They followed the Silk Road across the deserts of Central Asia on a journey which took them three years. They came back by sea, sailing down the coast of China, round the Malay Peninsula and the tip of India, to Persia. From there they travelled overland to the Mediterranean. Marco Polo wrote a book describing his travels and all the wonderful things he had seen, but for a long time few people believed his tales could possibly be true. From this time on other Europeans journeyed to the east. They all had to make the overland crossing through Arab lands, and travel by Arab ships.

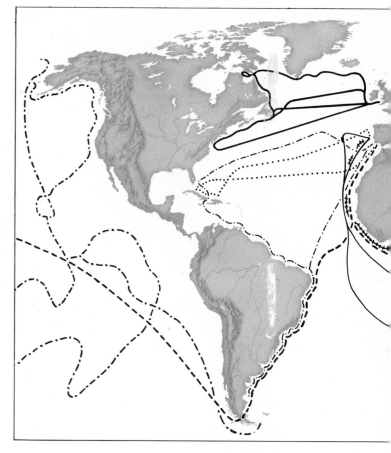

The voyages of some of the great explorers. For centuries one of the main reasons for their voyages was to try to find a quick way to the East. There they could buy cargoes of spices which they could sell at an enormous profit.

Sailing Round Africa

In the 1400s Portuguese sailors began to sail farther and farther down the west coast of Africa. They were helped by a group of mapmakers and astronomers, pilots and ship designers, who had been brought together by Prince Henry of Portugal. He is known as Prince Henry the Navigator. At first they hoped to gain control of the African gold trade from the Muslim merchants, and they built trading posts along the coast. There they exchanged horses, cloth, and brassware for gold dust, slaves, and ivory. Later their aims changed. They decided to try to sail south round Africa into the Indian Ocean and on to India. There they could buy the spices which fetched such high prices in Europe.

The first person to round the tip of Africa was Bartolomeu Dias, in 1487. Ten years later Vasco da Gama set out from Portugal to sail to the East. He rounded the tip of Africa, the Cape of Good Hope, and sailed northwards. Soon he reached an area where there were many Arab boats sailing from the east coast of Africa to India, and he collected an Arab pilot to show him the way. He sailed across the Indian Ocean to Calicut on the Indian coast. There he collected a cargo of spices and precious stones. His cargo was worth 60 times the cost of his expedition, but three-quarters of his crew died from disease on the voyage.

A New World in the West

Meanwhile, other explorers decided to try to reach the Spice Islands by sailing west. They never dreamt that a huge continent lay in their way. In 1492 Christopher Columbus, an Italian working for the Spanish queen,

Columbus's ship the *Santa Maria* was only 35 metres long. It had both square and triangular sails. Ships like this were used by most of the early explorers.

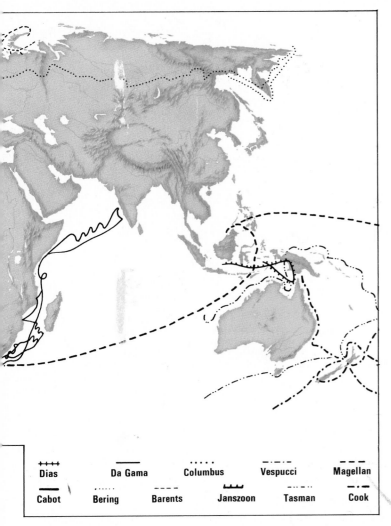

new continent had been discovered. It was named after the explorer Amerigo Vespucci who sailed far down the coast of Brazil. People also realized that they must find a way round America if they wanted to sail west to the Indies. In 1519 Ferdinand Magellan set out from Spain with five old ships. When he reached America he turned south, and then west through the strait which is called after him. For 38 days he steered through reefs and islands, with icy mountains towering above him. Then his ships reached a vast, calm ocean which he named the Pacific (peaceful) Ocean.

Magellan's ships sailed on across the open sea to the Philippines. There he was killed in a fight between the islanders. Only one ship of his five finally reached Spain, nearly three years later. It had made the first journey round the world, but it had also shown that the westward route to the Spice Islands was far too difficult and dangerous for ordinary trade.

Europeans in the East

East of India lay the Spice Islands or East Indies. They were the real centre of trade in the East. Most of the spices grew in the islands, and merchants from China, India, Persia, and Arabia sailed there to exchange their goods.

The first Europeans to reach the Spice Islands were the Portuguese. They soon captured the most important trading centres. Then they sailed to Canton, on the coast of China, and in the 1540s they landed in Japan. They were the first Europeans ever to reach there.

The Chinese did not want to have much to do with Europeans. They were not interested in buying European goods, though they would sell them silks and porcelain for gold. At first the Japanese were more welcoming. Christian missionaries followed the traders to Japan and taught many people their faith. But the rulers of Japan thought this was a threat to the Japanese way of life. They decided to cut their country off from almost all dealings with foreigners except for the Chinese, and for one Dutch ship a year.

set out with three little ships. After sailing for more than a month without sight of land, he reached the islands of the West Indies. He made four voyages altogether, sailing through the islands to the coasts of South and Central America. To the end of his life, he believed he had reached Asia; and this is why those islands are named the West Indies, and the people there and on the mainland of America became known as Indians.

Within a few years, other explorers sailed to America and people began to realize the truth. A vast

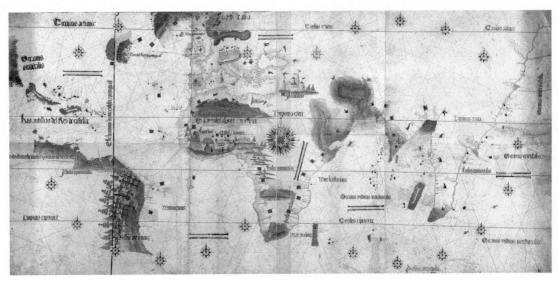

This map was drawn in 1502, only five years after Vasco da Gama set out to sail to India. Already the mapmakers can show Africa as pretty much the right shape. India looks rather strange and it is clear that the mapmakers had little knowledge of anywhere farther east. To the west, they show the West Indies and part of the South American coast.

49

The New World

Christopher Columbus reached America in 1492. Within a few years many other Europeans, eager to make their fortunes, arrived in the New World, as they called North and South America and the West Indies. The Spaniards and Portuguese considered that the New World was their territory.

The Spaniards flocked to Mexico and Peru. The Aztecs and the Incas (see page 44) did not stand a chance against the Spaniards, with their horses, armour, steel swords, and guns. By the middle 1500s the Spaniards had wiped out the great empires. They made slaves of the people, and forced them on pain of death to become Christians. Untold numbers of these Indians died from European diseases such as measles and smallpox, or from overwork and cruelty.

The other nations of Europe did not agree that the New World should belong to Spain. Soon they were attacking Spanish ships that were sailing home to Europe, laden with gold, silver, pearls, and emeralds. At first these buccaneers had the support of their governments, who were pleased to see Spain in trouble and to share in the profits. Later the buccaneers, safe in the bases they set up in the Caribbean islands, turned to outright piracy, attacking trading ships of all nations.

Farmers also went to the New World. They grew the local crops but they also took with them European plants and animals. Those settling in Central and South America were Spaniards and Portuguese. Farther north were English, French, and Dutch

This map of about 1540 shows the French explorer Jacques Cartier and his men in Canada. Cartier was sent by the French King Francis I to look for a way of sailing north-west around America to reach the East. He never discovered such a route, but as he searched for it he explored the coast of Canada and discovered the St Lawrence river.

This painting of an Indian village, Pomeiooc, dates from about 1585. It is one of several done by an Englishman called John White, who led an expedition to found a colony on the island of Roanoke, in what is now North Carolina. It failed because it included too many adventurers hoping to find gold, and too few genuine settlers. The first successful English settlement was in 1607.

settlers. Among the earliest settlers in North America were the Pilgrim Fathers. They sailed there from England because they could not worship God as they wanted to in Europe. They were soon followed by others. A number of French people went to what is now Canada. Many of them were trappers, catching animals like beavers and foxes for the fur trade. Then they explored south, along the rivers that lay west of the English and Dutch settlements. They claimed Louisiana, along the river Mississippi, for France.

The Indian Problem

The Indians who first met the European settlers in North America were farmers and hunters. Some tribes got on well with the settlers, even showing them what local plants and animals were good to eat. But as more and more settlers arrived from Europe, looking for land to farm, the Indians were in the way. There were battles. The Indians here, as in South America, died in large numbers from European diseases such as measles. Others moved away. Gradually the east coast colonies were cleared of Indians.

Meanwhile, the arrival of Europeans brought another, quite unforeseen change to the Indians' way of life. The Spaniards brought horses over with them, some of which strayed away and lived wild. Before long, great herds of wild horses grew up. Many Indians, who had been farmers, captured the horses. Now they could roam freely across the Great Plains of the Mid West. They became hunters, wandering after the great herds of buffalo that became their main source of food, and of leather for clothes and tents.

CANADA

GREAT LAKES

St Lawrence

•Montreal

•Plymouth

•New York

•Jamestown

ROCKY MOUNTAINS

GREAT PLAINS

Missouri

Mississippi

MEXICO

•Mexico City

WEST INDIES

Haiti

CARIBBEAN SEA

Amazon

PERU

ANDES MOUNTAINS

BRAZIL

•Rio de Janeiro

Buenos Aires•

Early Puritan settlers in North America. They went there from England so that they could worship God in the way they wanted.

Negro slaves working on a sugar cane plantation. Sugar cane was taken to the Americas from the Old World, and soon became a very important crop there.

Settlers in the North

In the colonies on the east coast of North America two different ways of life gradually grew up. In the more northern states, people mostly worked their own small farms, or were trappers or traders. But farther south, people owned much larger estates. There they would grow one main crop such as sugar, cotton, or tobacco. The same sort of crops were grown on the islands of the West Indies. Work on the estates was hard and the climate was hot. European workers did not want to work there. A terrible answer was found to this problem. European merchants sailed to West Africa, where they bought or captured slaves. They shipped them across the Atlantic under appalling conditions, and sold them in the West Indies. Over 10 million slaves were taken to the Americas before the trade was stopped in the 1800s.

The *conquistadors,* as the Spaniards who conquered South and Central America and the West Indies are known, soon needed men to work on the land and in the mines. Here a group of conquistadors, on the left, watches slaves brought from Africa at work in the silver mines of Haiti.

A Spanish conquistador.

The Renaissance and the Reformation

In the 15th century Italian artists, sculptors, architects, and scholars all became fascinated by the arts and learning of Ancient Greece and Rome. We call this renewal of interest the *Renaissance*, which means the rebirth. At this time many of the Italian cities had grown very wealthy through trade. The rich people who lived there wanted paintings and statues to make their houses beautiful. Until then, artists and sculptors had been craftsmen, expected to follow the usual rather flat and stiff-looking styles. Now they studied ancient art and then tried to make their own pictures and statues look as lifelike. Instead of showing only religious subjects, they began to produce works showing scenes from history and legend, and important recent events. Architects followed the proportions and pillars of Greek buildings and the domes and arches of Roman buildings to make a beautiful new style of their own.

For a long time learning had been controlled by the Church. Now people were becoming interested in old books and were studying not only Latin but Greek and Hebrew as well. People became very interested in experimenting and finding out about the world around them. Some of their findings about the Sun, planets, and stars got them into trouble with the Church, because they went against what people then believed to be true.

The new interest in art and learning spread out across Europe. It was helped by the invention of printing in the 1450s. This meant that books setting out new ideas could quickly and easily be read by many people.

Questioning the Church

This wish to talk over problems and look for ways of solving them spilt over into Church matters. People began to look at the Church and the way it was run. They found many things to criticize. They could see that their highly organized and very wealthy Church was far different from the Church of the early Christians. It was also true that not all priests, monks, and nuns kept their vows to live lives serving God.

One man who was particularly upset by the things he found wrong with the Church was a German monk named Martin Luther. He hoped to talk over ways of reforming the Church, but many people naturally resented his criticisms and attacked his ideas. While he defended himself, Luther realized that he even disagreed with some of the things the Church taught about Christ. Luther might have been burned as a heretic, as other critics before him had been, but he had a great deal of support. This came not only from ordinary people, but from princes too.

In the end, the Church split in two. Those people who followed Luther and protested that changes were needed were known as Protestants. Those who remained faithful to the old Church were called Roman Catholics. Soon Protestant groups grew up in

This picture was painted by the Italian artist Gozzoli in 1459. It is part of a picture showing the Wise Men, or Magi, who visited Jesus. Instead of painting a scene in the Bible Lands, with eastern figures of the time, the artist has painted members of the Medici family. They were rich bankers, several of whom ruled the city of Florence during the Renaissance. The young man on the white horse is Lorenzo de Medici, who was known as Lorenzo the Magnificent. He was a famous statesman and a good architect, and he wrote poetry and songs. He encouraged people to learn about art and science. Florence was one of the great Renaissance centres of learning and art, and this lifelike painting shows the style in which artists of the time were working.

many parts of Europe. Many German princes supported Luther because they wanted to seize lands belonging to the Church. War broke out between them and the Catholic countries. Neither side won a clear victory, so the Holy Roman Emperor had to allow the ruler of each state to decide whether his country should be Catholic or Protestant. Meanwhile, the leaders of the Catholic Church called a great council to work out how they could make their Church better.

Rulers did not believe their subjects could be loyal unless they were all of the same religion. And rulers tended to make alliances with other rulers of the same faith. As a result, wars broke out over religion not just inside countries, but between countries too. These included the Thirty Years' War, from 1618 to 1648. The Protestants from Germany and Scandinavia

The wars of religion which were fought in Europe in the late 1500s and early 1600s were carried out with very great cruelty. Much of the fighting was in Germany. Farmland was destroyed and villages and towns were burned and looted. Here a group of soldiers attacks a family of farmers.

fought the Catholics of Germany, Austria, and Spain. Catholic France joined in on the side of the Protestants to prevent Spain and Austria getting more powerful. By the end of the war, Germany was split into mainly Protestant north, with Catholic states in the west and south. Protestant Holland was given independence from Spanish rule. But the war left many countries very poor, and much of Germany had been ruined by the many battles fought there.

The Church in England

The Church of England split away from the Roman Catholic Church because the king did not want to obey the Pope, the Catholic Church's leader, who forbade him to divorce his wife. He declared that he himself was head of the Church in England. The English sided with the Protestants, even though they had rather different beliefs.

Martin Luther was a German monk who criticized the Roman Catholic Church. He set up his own organization of Christians in Germany, and he and his followers became known as Protestants because they protested against some of the ways and beliefs of the Catholic Church. The Protestants believed that the words of the Bible should be studied very carefully. They handed out copies of the Bible in a German translation so that ordinary German Christians could read it for themselves. Many small states in northern Europe became Protestant.

This map shows Roman Catholic and Protestant parts of northern Europe in 1550. The cream-coloured area on the right was mixed. At first the Protestants gained enormous numbers of supporters all over northern Europe and France, but by now the Catholic Church had won many people back.

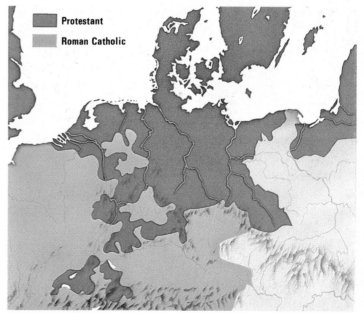

Protestant

Roman Catholic

Captain Cook and the Pacific

By the 1750s explorers had mapped the coasts of North and South America, Asia, Europe, and Africa. But one great area of the world was still almost unknown. This was the South Pacific, and in it the great continent of Australia.

Dutch sailors blown west from the tip of South Africa discovered the north and west coasts of Australia by accident in the 1600s. These were dry, rocky areas and the sailors soon went on to the Spice Islands. Later that century Abel Tasman sailed right round Australia without realizing it was there, although he landed on the island called Tasmania after him. When he reached New Zealand he believed he had found part of a huge mass of land, which people thought lay south of Africa and the tip of South America. It was known as *Terra Australis Incognita*, the Latin for 'the unknown land to the south'.

Voyage to the South

In 1768 an English sailor, James Cook, was sent to look for this great southern land. He sailed to New Zealand, which he claimed for Britain. He made maps of its two islands, and then sailed on to reach the east coast of Australia. He made maps of this, too, while artists and naturalists on his ship drew pictures and wrote records of all the strange plants and animals they saw. Cook made three long journeys to the South Pacific. He showed that there was no great land mass, but instead the huge island of Australia. On his last voyage he was killed in a quarrel with the people of Hawaii, who were tired of the visits of English sailors asking them for food.

Cook claimed much of eastern Australia for Britain. He called it New South Wales. In 1788 the first British settlers arrived there. They were convicts and their guards. Soon free settlers arrived to farm the land. Then gold was discovered. In the 1850s people rushed to Australia from all over the world, hoping to find gold and make their fortunes. Many who did not find gold stayed on to farm or to work in the growing towns. By the end of the 1800s there were a number of different British colonies in Australia. In 1901 they became states and joined together to make up the Commonwealth of Australia.

Cook's ship *Endeavour*.

Cook's ship *Endeavour* was little bigger than the ships of the great Portuguese explorers (see page 48). He had better instruments to help him find out exactly where he was. One of these was a special kind of watch called a *chronometer*. It kept time much more accurately than any ordinary watch or clock and Cook was one of the first people to test it out on a long voyage. If someone knew exactly when midday was in London, he could work out how different it was in local time and that told him how far east or west he was. An instrument called a sextant measured the Sun's position in the sky, which told him how far north or south he was. This was invented 50 years before Cook's voyages. He also used the compass. Its needle always pointed north, and sailors had used it since the 1100s to see which way they were going.

Great Sandy Desert

Dampier

Gulf of Carpentaria

AUSTRALIA

Great Dividing Range

Great Victoria Desert

Darling

Perth

Great Australian Bight

Murrumbidgee

Adelaide

Murray

Sydney
Botany Bay

Melbourne

Captain Cook took very good care of his crew. In his time sailors often had bad food to eat and lived in dirty quarters. Many of them got serious illnesses because of this. Captain Cook made sure that his crew ate sauerkraut (a kind of pickled cabbage), fruit and carrots to keep them healthy. He also made them keep their living quarters clean and aired.

Kangaroos were among the many strange animals which Cook and his crew found in Australia.

A man from Cook's ship draws a strange plant. At one landing in Australia, Cook's party found so many new plants that he named the place Botany Bay.

TASMANIA

(Van Diemen's Land)

Russell

NEW ZEALAND

North Island

Wellington

South Island

Dunedin

New Zealand

Cook was the first European to land in New Zealand. Tasman had tried to land more than a hundred years before, but had been driven off by the fierce Maori people who lived there. Cook never quarrelled with them but other explorers were less lucky, and New Zealand was known far and wide for its fierce people. The first settlers from Britain did not arrive until 1840. They began to farm the rich country, buying land from the Maoris. This led to quarrels and there was war between the Maoris and the white settlers. Peace was made in 1870 and since that time New Zealand has been a peaceful farming country.

Cook's voyages across the Pacific opened up the area to Europeans. First France, and later Germany and the United States, joined Britain in taking control of groups of Pacific islands. Missionaries converted the islanders to Christianity and taught them European ways, while traders grew rich from the fertilizers and coconut oil they sent back.

When Cook landed in New Zealand he was met by the warlike Maoris. They were a frightening sight with their tattooed faces. They paddled war canoes with carved prows. Cook got on well with them and they let him map their islands. The little map shows Cook's voyages.

The Empire Builders

The great empires of the Ancient World and the Middle Ages grew up as powerful states gained control of their neighbours. This was the way in which Russia built up an empire, spreading eastwards right across northern Asia in the 1500s, 1600s, and 1700s. But at the same time a different sort of empire was growing up, as Europeans spread out all over the world. These new empires were scattered over far distant continents, often many weeks' journey from their mother countries.

New-World Empires
The first Europeans to reach Central and South America soon conquered the people living there, who had little defence against the well armed and armoured invaders. The Europeans took the Indians' lands and made them work on the plantations and in the silver mines. They brought slaves from Africa as extra labour. The Indians of North America managed to destroy some of the early colonies set up there by the Dutch, French, and English, and fought fiercely for hundreds of years. But eventually the Europeans controlled the whole country. In Australia and New Zealand, too, the British took the country over.

Today these countries are independent. But most of the people there are descended wholly or partly from Europeans. They speak the languages of the early settlers: Spanish and Portuguese in Central and South America, English in Australia and New Zealand, the United States and part of Canada, and French in the rest of Canada. Most of their ways of life, too, developed from those of their mother countries.

Traders in the East
The Europeans who sailed to the East found a very different state of affairs. There was no question of defeating almost defenceless local people and taking over their land. Instead, the Europeans had to trade in competition with merchants from all over Asia, who laughed at the poor quality of European goods and would trade only for gold and silver. Local rulers laid down the conditions of trading.

The first Europeans to arrive in the East were the Portuguese. They came to trade and not to build an empire, but soon they decided to take control of the 'spice route' along which their ships sailed. They had good ships and firearms. Within a few years they had taken over a string of ports: Mozambique on the east coast of Africa; Ormuz at the mouth of the Arabian/Persian Gulf; Goa on the coast of India; the port of Malacca on the Malay Peninsula; and the Spice Islands themselves. Now they controlled the main

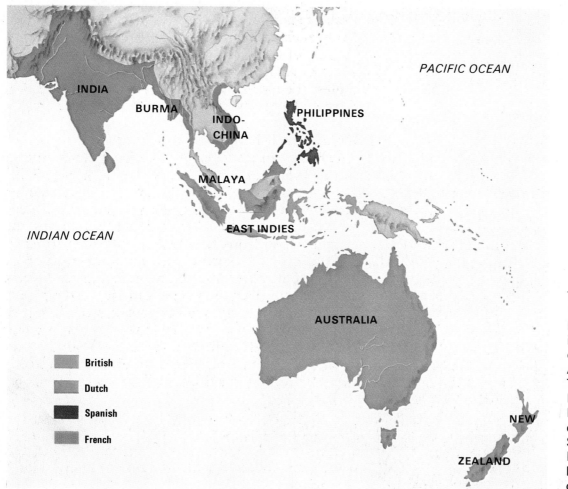

British
Dutch
Spanish
French

This map shows the East in 1878. By this time Britain had built up a great empire including India, Burma, parts of Malaya and Borneo, Australia and New Zealand. The Dutch ruled the East Indies (Indonesia) and the French had recently taken over 'Indochina'. The Spanish still ruled the Philippines, but 20 years later the United States gained control of them.

Soldiers of the Indian Army in 1902. India was divided into provinces each ruled by a British governor, and states ruled by Indian princes. They let the British manage their foreign affairs in return for military protection. In 1878 Queen Victoria was proclaimed Empress of India, and she took a great interest in the country. The Indian Army included British and Indian officers and Indian soldiers from all parts of the country. They fought bravely for Britain in both the First and Second World Wars.

centres for collecting and trading in spices. They made a great deal of money from trading between the ports. Meanwhile the Spanish took over the Philippines. They sailed there from Mexico with cargoes of silver, which they exchanged for silk from China.

Before long the Dutch, English, and then the French sailed on to the scene. They set up East India companies to organize trading and settlements. The Dutch, who had better ships, drove the Portuguese from the Spice Islands. They too wanted simply to control trading stations and the routes between them. But soon the local rulers gave the Dutch land in return for protection, and a Dutch empire grew up. Dutch settlers began to grow tea and coffee, sugar and

This bridge is typically Dutch – but it is in Djakarta, on the island of Java in Indonesia. The Dutch ruled these islands for several hundred years.

tobacco there as well as spices, all of which were shipped back to Europe.

The French and British settled in trading posts around the coasts of India, with the permission of the Mughal emperors. At first these powerful rulers could easily have driven the Europeans out, but in the 1700s they became weak. To safeguard their trade, the Europeans employed soldiers and made treaties with the local rulers. When war broke out between the British and French in Europe, they fought too in India. The British were able to control shipping, so French soldiers and supplies could not reach India. The British, under their brilliant general Robert Clive, took over the French settlements in India. A number of treaties with local rulers gave the British control over most of India, and to protect their trade routes, the British took over Aden in the Red Sea, Burma, the Malay States, Penang, and Singapore.

Running the Empires

The European countries did well from their empires. Trade with them brought a great deal of money. Some of the Europeans were cruel masters. They made the local people work for long hours in hard conditions, for very low pay. But others did their best to help the people whose lands they controlled. They tried to keep peace and spread law and order, without upsetting local customs. They built dams and roads and railways. They dug wells and taught the people new ways of farming, and built schools and hospitals for them. They honestly thought that they were doing good by spreading European laws, customs, and religion. Many of them lived lonely and dangerous lives, far from other Europeans, as they carried out their duty.

When these countries became independent again, most of the Europeans went home. They left behind a framework of government and communications, and of western skills, which the new countries could use if they wished to.

Across the World

When the first Europeans reached America in the 1490s and 1500s they found many plants and animals there which they had not seen before. Before long they brought them back to Europe and began growing them there. At the same time, they took plants and animals from Europe and Asia to the New World. Later they introduced new plants and animals to Australia and Africa.

Some of these plants and animals are so successful in their new homes that it is hard to remember that they have not always been there. Crops like wheat in America, maize in Africa, and potatoes in Europe are a

Horses were found in the New World in prehistoric times, but they died out there long before Europeans arrived. The early Spaniards took horses with them. Some of these escaped and before long large herds of wild horses grew up. These were the horses ridden by the American Indians.

Potatoes were brought to Europe from Peru and Chile in the late 1500s. A hundred years later they were a major crop in Ireland, and by the late 1700s they were grown all over Europe, especially in England and Germany. European settlers took potatoes to North America, southern Africa, and Australasia.

Rice was introduced to southern Europe by the Arabs in the Middle Ages. Europeans took it to the Americas and by 1850 it was well established in the southern states of North America.

Spanish and Portuguese explorers took **wheat** to the Americas in the 1500s. It is now a very important crop there, and in Australia.

Coffee spread from Ethiopia to southern Arabia in about 1500. From there it spread through Africa and Asia, and Europeans took it to Central and South America. The largest producer today is Brazil.

Columbus took **sugar cane** to the West Indies in 1493 and soon after Europeans took it to Central and South America. By 1600 it was grown in all the tropical countries of the Americas and by 1817 it was growing in Australia.

Tomatoes come from South America. Although Europeans brought them home in the 1500s it was a long time before they were widely eaten. For 200 years or so they were grown as a curiosity!

Soon after America was discovered in 1492 Europeans took **banana** plants from the Canary Islands to the West Indies. From here they quickly spread to the American mainland. Now they are widely grown in Central and South America and in Australia.

CANADA

NORTH AMERICA

EUR

Canary
Islands

AFRICA

West Indies

CENTRAL AMERICA

Brazil

SOUTH AMERICA

major part of people's everyday food. Others are very important to the new region's economy, like coffee in Brazil and ground nuts in Africa. Sometimes people have developed special breeds of animals and plants to suit their new homes.

Peoples as well as plants and animals have moved from one continent to another. Europeans have spread all over the world; Negroes from Africa make up an important part of the American population. More recently people from Asia have spread over the world, sometimes seeking work and sometimes as refugees.

Maize grows in America from Canada south to Chile. The Spaniards and Portuguese brought it back to the Old World. By 1650 it was growing all over southern Europe and in Africa, India, Tibet, and China. Now it is one of the most widely grown of all food crops.

RUSSIA

CENTRAL ASIA

Turkey

Egypt

Arabia

TIBET

CHINA

Japan

INDIA

Columbus brought **cocoa** back from America to Spain in 1502, but it could not be grown there. In the early 1900s the countries of tropical Africa became the leading cocoa producers and still produce much of the world's supply. Today cocoa is also grown in Papua-New Guinea and the Solomon Islands.

Sri Lanka

Malaya

Rubber comes originally from Central and South America. In the late 1800s plants and seeds were brought back to Britain, and from there they were taken to Ceylon, India, and Malaya, and other parts of the East. Before long more rubber was produced there than in the Americas.

Papua-New Guinea

Solomon Islands

AUSTRALIA

Tobacco was brought to Europe from America in the 1500s but only a little was grown there. Its cultivation spread in the 1800s to more than 90 countries, including Turkey, India, mainland China, and Japan. In the 1900s tobacco growing has become very important in south-central Africa.

Sheep and **cattle** were taken to the New World and Australasia by the Europeans. Special breeds have been developed which are well suited to these countries, where they are kept in enormous quantities.

NEW ZEALAND

59

Revolutions and Nationalism

During the 1500s, 1600s, and 1700s Europeans explored the world and built up great empires. At home, most of their countries were ruled by powerful kings or emperors and ordinary people had little or no say in how things were run. But during the 1700s some people began to think that everyone had the right to a say in how they were governed.

In the 1770s a number of Britain's colonies in America decided that they wanted to govern themselves. They felt that it was unfair for the British Parliament to make laws for them and tax them without consulting them. The colonies declared themselves independent, and after some fierce battles they defeated the British. They formed a new republic which they called the United States of America.

This was the first of many rebellions. Some of them were against foreign rulers, and others were against harsh and unfair governments. The poor people of France were taxed so heavily and had so few rights that they rose up against their rulers. During the French Revolution, as their rebellion is called, their king and queen and many nobles were executed. A general called Napoleon came to power. He conquered an empire stretching over most of Europe, and turned several rulers off their thrones. Napoleon himself was finally defeated in 1815 at the battle of Waterloo. The kings he had deposed took up rule again. But people now realized that rulers and frontiers could be changed. During the 1800s many countries fought for and gained their independence, and the peace treaties after the First World War gave still more the freedom to rule themselves.

In the early 1900s the people of Russia were ruled by the Tsar, who had complete power over his vast, backward country. Most of the people were desper-ately poor and had no education. In 1917 the Tsar was overthrown and he and his family were later murdered. The Communists seized power. The German and Austrian Empires were abolished after the first World War. The imperial rulers of Europe had finally been swept away.

Peaceful Revolutions

Meanwhile, another sort of revolution was taking place. The invention of steam engines led to new, bigger machines and the growth of large industries, first in Britain and then in many other countries. This brought many changes in the way in which people lived, gathering them in crowded and dirty towns. Perhaps the greatest change of all was brought about by new kinds of transport and communications. These made it possible for people to travel long distances quickly and easily, and to speak to people on the other side of the world. By the end of the 1800s, events in one country could affect places across the Earth. The world seemed to be growing smaller.

Napoleon and his army on their retreat from Moscow. After the turmoil of the French Revolution, Napoleon took over the rule of France and in 1804 proclaimed himself emperor. He raised a huge citizen army, for which all childless men between 18 and 40 could be called up. With it he conquered a great European empire, bringing Spain, Italy, Germany and part of Poland under his control. He made alliances with Austria and Prussia after defeating them. He was determined to add Russia to his empire and in June 1812 he invaded it with 600,000 men. He captured Moscow, which the Russians had set on fire, but as the bitterly cold Russian winter set in he had to retreat. The terrible cold, lack of food or shelter, and constant attacks by the Russians meant that only 100,000 of his men survived.

IMPORTANT DATES

1733 John Kay produced his 'flying shuttle', the first important textile invention, to speed up weaving. Soon other machines were invented which were powered first by water and later by steam.

1776 Thirteen British colonies in North America declared their independence. War followed until in 1783 the British recognized the independence of the new United States of America.

1789 The French Revolution broke out. At first it was orderly; power was given to a new Assembly of commoners which brought in many reforms. In 1792 the monarchy was abolished and a republic set up. The king was tried and executed. Civil war broke out, and anyone found guilty of opposing the Republic was executed. Eventually the leader of this 'Reign of Terror' was executed, and order was gradually restored.

1799 Napoleon Bonaparte took power in France as First Consul. In 1804 he crowned himself Emperor. In a series of wars he gained control over much of Europe.

1804 Richard Trevithick developed the steam locomotive. From now on railways were built and spread all over the world.

1805 Napoleon's fleet was defeated by the British under Nelson at Trafalgar.

1806 Napoleon dissolved the Holy Roman Empire.

1813 A combined force of Austrians, Russians, and Prussians defeated the French at the battle of Leipzig; the British drove the French out of Spain. The next year Napoleon abdicated and was exiled.

1815 Napoleon returned from exile and raised an army. This was defeated by the British and Prussians at Waterloo.

1819 Simón Bolívar led New Granada, in South America, to independence from Spain. From this time on the other South American countries gained independence from Spain and Portugal.

1830 Greece became independent from Turkey. Belgium broke away from the Netherlands to become independent.

1837 Queen Victoria came to the throne of Britain. Her reign, which lasted until 1901, saw Britain reach the height of its power and wealth at home and in its Empire. In the same year Samuel Morse invented the telegraph.

1845 A disastrous blight ruined most of the potato crop in Ireland. The next year the crop was even worse. Some four million poor people there lived almost entirely on potatoes, and perhaps a million died during this famine. During the next 15 years about a million Irish people emigrated to the United States.

1848 This is often called the 'Year of Revolutions'. Revolution in France overthrew its king and set up a second Republic under Napoleon's nephew Louis Napoleon. There were unsuccessful risings against the governments and rulers in Italy, Hungary, and Germany.

1854 The Crimean War broke out between Russia and Turkey which was backed by Britain and France. The Russians had invaded Turkish land as they wanted to be the most influential power in the Ottoman Empire. The war ended with Russian defeat in 1856. Disease caused more deaths than fighting but British hospitals were set up under Florence Nightingale.

1854 The American Matthew Perry landed in Japan and forced the Japanese to open their country to foreign trade.

1857 Mutiny broke out in India when native soldiers rebelled against the British. Peace was restored in 1858.

1861 The Kingdom of Italy was proclaimed after Garibaldi handed Naples and Sicily to the king of Piedmont.

1861 Civil War broke out in America between the states of the North and South. It lasted until 1865 when the North won. All slaves were freed.

1869 The Suez Canal was opened, joining the Mediterranean to the Red Sea and shortening the journey to the East by thousands of kilometres.

1871 Germany was united as an empire under the king of Prussia.

1876 The telephone was invented by Alexander Graham Bell.

1884 At the Berlin Conference the important European countries laid down ground rules for their partition of Africa.

1887 The invention of the motor-car engine led to a second great transport revolution.

1895 Marconi developed his system of 'wireless telegraphy' or radio.

1899 War broke out between the British and the Boers (Dutch-descended settlers) in South Africa. The British took over the Boer republics and in 1910 the Union of South Africa was formed.

1900 Chinese nationalists attacked Europeans in several Chinese towns and besieged them for 55 days in Peking. More than 200 Europeans were killed and their countrymen took harsh measures against the Chinese in return.

1903 The first powered flight was made by the Wright brothers in North Carolina.

1904 War broke out between Russia and Japan. The Russians were shamingly defeated.

1905 Revolution in Russia was halted when the Tsar granted some reforms.

1914 The outbreak of the First World War.

The Industrial Revolution

Two revolutions began in Britain in the 1700s that made great changes in people's lives and surroundings. The first revolution was in farming. Until then, farming had changed little since the Middle Ages (see page 38). But now people gave up their strips of land and share of common land in return for land all in one place. Landowners fenced in large areas of what had been common lands. New crops like turnips and clover were grown and fertilizers were used so better crops were produced. Fields did not need now to be left fallow for one year in every three. New farmland was won by draining marshy country.

At the same time extra care was taken with animals. The new crops provided food to keep all animals through the winter, and the very best animals were chosen to breed from. This produced better animals, that gave more meat or wool. Inventors made machines to help with hoeing, sowing seeds, and spreading manure. The result of all this meant better farming and more food.

Canals and Coal

The second revolution was in transport and industry. It was very expensive to carry heavy goods by road. Water transport was cheaper, but rivers did not always go to the right places. Now canals were built so that heavy goods could be taken cheaply to large cities. Ways were found to build good roads with hard surfaces, so travel by coach and cart speeded up, although it was still expensive.

Above: New ways of farming brought great prosperity to landowners, but villagers who could no longer graze their animals on common land suffered. Many of them went to work in the new towns which grew up round the factories. The houses they lived in there were often no smaller than the houses in the villages, but they were crowded together and very unhealthy.

Women at work in a textile mill in the early 1800s. The textile industry was the first to use heavy machines in factories. At first these were driven by water but later steam engines were used. The machines were dangerous and many of the workers were injured by them.

The iron industry in Britain was quite small. The problem was that charcoal made from wood was used to smelt iron, and wood was becoming scarcer. Coal could not be used, because its gases made iron brittle. In the 1700s people found out how to turn coal into coke. This could be used to make iron. Other changes in iron making meant that ironmasters could produce large quantities of good quality iron quickly and cheaply. People began to use iron for making bridges, machines, ships, and many other things. By 1800 Britain produced more iron and coal than all the rest of the world together.

Steam Power

In the early 1700s people began to make machines driven by the power of steam. At first it was only used to drive machines like pumps, with an up and down movement. Later people found out how to drive wheels round as well, so many different kinds of

machine could be steam driven. Now they began to think of using steam to make engines travel. They put a moving engine on a track of rails and the railway was born. This made travel quick and cheap for people and goods.

Until the mid 1700s the making of cloth was done mostly by villagers, who spun yarn and wove cloth in their cottages. Then machines were invented that were driven first by water wheels, and then by the new steam engines. They could do the work of many people, very quickly and cheaply. Clever men made huge profits by building factories housing such machines. The use of machines and factories soon spread to other industries.

People flocked to work in the new factories. Many were small farmers and craftsmen who had been ruined because they could neither afford to take up the new ways, nor compete with them. New cities were quickly built, but they were filthy and unhealthy. No one controlled the smoke and dirt coming from the factories. The houses for the workers were small and crowded together and many of the people living there became ill. Working conditions in the factories and the mines were appalling, and men, women, and children had to work very long hours there.

All through the 1800s reformers fought to get better working conditions. Others tried to get help for those who had become poor through no fault of their own. They had to go to a workhouse where conditions were so bad that it was as if poor, unemployed, old, and sick

people, and orphans were punished for their troubles, rather than helped. Workers tried to help themselves by forming trade unions that fought for better conditions.

Britain was the first country to have an industrial revolution, but soon other countries followed. In the late 1800s came another wave of changes. Steel, made mainly in Germany and the United States, replaced iron. The chemical industry grew up, producing dyes and drugs, explosives and fibres from coal. New sources of power, such as electricity and petrol which was used to fuel the internal combustion engine were developed. Many new inventions followed, and people's lives changed more and more.

At work in a coal mine in the early 1800s. Coal was used as fuel for steam engines and blast furnaces. Conditions in the mines were very bad, and men, women, and children worked for long hours there.

Independence in the Americas

In 1776, 13 British colonies in North America declared themselves independent. They fought against their British rulers, and set up their own republic of the United States of America. Before long, other colonies in the Americas were following their example.

Much of Central and South America was part of the Spanish empire. It was ruled by Spaniards *from Spain*. Spaniards who had been born in the Americas, who were known as Creoles, were kept out of power. The successful revolution in North America encouraged the Creoles to fight for their own independence in the early 1800s. In the north, they were led by Simón Bolívar, the son of a Creole landowner. He knew that he and his followers could never beat the Spanish troops in battle. Instead Bolívar and his followers, who knew the countryside well, fought a *guerilla* war. They attacked small groups of Spanish soldiers and prevented them from joining into a large army. After several years of fighting Bolívar freed the north from Spanish rule. Meanwhile, the Creoles in Mexico rose up to free themselves, and in the south José de San Martín led the people to drive out the Spaniards.

Brazil was ruled by the Portuguese. When Portugal was overrun by Napoleon's armies, its royal family escaped to Brazil. They grew to like the country. After the king returned to Portugal, his son declared Brazil independent. Eventually it became a republic.

Many of the people of South America were little better off after independence. Creoles replaced the Spaniards as rulers, but the lives of the peasants (many of whom were of mixed Spanish and Indian blood) remained very hard.

The Move West

The 13 colonies which formed the United States of America all lay on or near the east coast. To the north were the colonies of Canada, which had stayed loyal to the British. West and south were French and Spanish lands, and vast areas of mountain and plain lived in by Indians. These were visited by only a few European fur trappers and traders. In the next hundred years the United States spread across North America. It bought Louisiana, the region round the Mississippi River, from France. It won lands in the south and west from Mexico and Spain.

Pioneers moved westwards to settle the new lands. They travelled with all their possessions in processions of covered waggons. Most of them were farmers, in search of new, cheap land. They had to be tough and self-reliant. Their journey might last many months, and took them through mountain ranges and across the Great Plains, where dust was whirled round them in summer and in winter they were frozen by blizzards. They also were attacked by the Indians, whose land they were taking. After they settled down and began to farm, Indians often stole their crops and cattle, and burnt their homes.

In 1848 gold was discovered in California, on the west coast. Hundreds of thousands of people moved there in a great 'gold rush'. Railways were built to bring them supplies of food and equipment, and by 1869 a railway stretched right across the continent from east to west. It crossed the Great Plains, lived in only by Indians, who hunted the huge herds of buffalo which roamed there. The white men soon wiped out these herds, and the Indians lost their source of food. By 1890, the Indians and the buffalo were found only in special reservations. The Plains were settled by farmers, who raised great herds of cattle and planted vast fields of wheat.

All through the 1800s, Europeans were sailing west to America. Some left their homes because of poor harvests and lack of work. Others had disagreed with the government. They settled in the United States, becoming farmers or working in the new industries that were growing up in the east. By 1900 the United States had become an important industrial nation, and soon it was to become one of the most powerful countries in the world.

A statue of the South American leader José de San Martín. He was born in Argentina and led it in its fight for independence from Spanish rule. He also helped Chile and Peru to gain their independence.

CANADA

GREAT PLAINS

ROCKY MOUNTAINS

California

UNITED STATES
OF AMERICA

● New York

Mississippi

MEXICO

Covered waggons, drawn
by oxen or horses, carried
pioneers westwards. They
depended on their skills as
farmers and hunters for
their survival.

The Confed   Army charges a ridge during the battle of
Gettysburg, in   American Civil War. This battle was won
by the Union Army which went on to win the War. It had
broken out between the Union (northern) and Confederate
(southern) states in 1861. The southern states depended on
plantations worked by black slaves, and the northern states
on industry without slaves. They quarrelled as to whether the
new states being formed should allow slavery or not. The
southern states separated to form a new nation, but the other
states would not agree to this and war broke out. It ended
four years later after over 600,000 people had been killed. All
slaves were given their freedom. The war made people in the
North and South feel very bitter towards one another.

BRAZIL

PERU

ANDES MOUNTAINS

BOLIVIA

CHILE

ARGENTINA

New Nations in Europe

At the beginning of the 1800s Britain, France, Spain, Portugal, and Switzerland had almost the same borders as they have today. But elsewhere in Europe things were rather different. Sprawling across central Europe was the Holy Roman Empire. It was made up of hundreds of little states, which were loosely linked under the leadership of the emperor of Austria, the great country in the south of the Empire. Italy too was made up of a number of small states, and much of south-east Europe was ruled by the Ottoman Turks.

The examples of the Americans, who had won their independence and become a nation, and of the French who had fought for a share in their own government, had a deep effect on many people in Europe. Some, like the Italians, dreamt of being a united nation. Others, who were ruled by foreigners, dreamt of being free and running their own separate country. These feelings are known as Nationalism and Nationalism showed itself in many ways. The first was people's new pride in and love of the country where they were born. This was followed by a new interest in their race

Left: Prince Otto von Bismarck became the chief minister of Prussia in 1862 and by clever scheming united the German states in a new German empire.

Right: Garibaldi led the Italians of Sicily and southern Italy to independence. He was the son of a fisherman, and spent some years in South America. When he came back to Italy and took up the fight for independence he became very popular.

and its history and past triumphs, its language and traditions, and its myths and legends. All these things inspired the writings of the 1800s and the music composed at that time.

With the new Nationalism often came demands that people should be allowed more say in the government of their countries. This naturally did not please the kings and nobles, who wanted to keep power for themselves. So both nationalists and people who wanted to reform governments often had to work in secret. There were plots and uprisings that failed, and many people died or were imprisoned for their beliefs.

The Ottoman Empire Breaks Up

In the 1800s the great Ottoman Empire grew too weak to keep its subject countries. In 1830 the Greeks broke free from the Ottomans. This gave hope to many other

A group of Wallachians in national dress, painted in 1860. They lived in the Balkans, which had been ruled by the Turks for hundreds of years as part of their Ottoman Empire. In the 1800s the Ottomans were weak and the Balkan countries fought for their independence. Wallachia joined Moldavia to form the new country of Romania in 1861. In 1878 the powerful European countries recognized Romania as completely independent from Turkey.

people in the Balkan Peninsula of south-east Europe, who were under Turkish rule. Many of these people were Slavs by race, and belonged to the Orthodox Christian Church. The same was true of the Russians, who helped them. In 1878 a great congress (meeting) of the important European countries was held in Berlin. They agreed that Serbia, Montenegro, and Romania should be independent. Soon other Balkan countries broke away from Turkey. In North Africa, too, the Ottoman Empire was breaking up, but there its lands were taken over by other imperial countries.

German and Italian Unity

The Holy Roman Empire was done away with by Napoleon in 1806, when he gained control of all its countries. The most powerful of its northern states, Prussia, began to form close links with the little states around it. In 1862 Prince Otto von Bismarck became the chief minister of Prussia. He persuaded or forced all the other little states to join Prussia. They became a new German empire, and the king of Prussia became their *Kaiser*, or emperor. Austria in the south had its own empire, together with Hungary which had long been ruled by the Habsburg emperors of Austria, although it was not part of the old Holy Roman Empire.

Meanwhile Italy, which had been divided between Austria, the Pope, and several other rulers, won its way to freedom and unity. In 1870 it became one kingdom under the king of Piedmont, the northern state which had led the others to join it and throw off their rulers.

The last of the great frontier changes took place after the First World War, which ended in 1918. The Austrian Empire was broken up, and Hungary and Czechoslovakia were formed. Some of the states in the Balkan peninsula were rearranged to make the modern countries of Yugoslavia, Romania, Bulgaria, and Albania. In the north, Poland, which had been divided between Russia, Prussia, and Austria, became free and independent once more. Europe had taken the shape we know today.

This map shows the Ottoman Empire, the Austrian Empire, Russia, and Prussia in colour, as they were in 1815. The red line shows the old Holy Roman Empire. The borders and names are those of today.
The Netherlands became independent from Spain in 1648. **Belgium**, ruled by Spain, Austria, and then France, was joined to the Netherlands in 1815 but broke away in 1830.
Czechoslovakia gained independence in 1918.
Hungary became a partner in the Austrian Empire in 1867, and independent in 1918.
Poland was divided between Prussia, Austria, and Russia in 1815. It was reunited as an independent country in 1918.
Yugoslavia was formed after the First World War. Parts of it had won freedom from the Ottoman Turks in the 1870s.
Romania's independence from the Ottomans was recognized in 1861. After the First World War lands from the Austro-Hungarian Empire, were joined to it.
Greece became an independent kingdom in 1830.
Bulgaria became independent in 1908 and **Albania** in 1912.

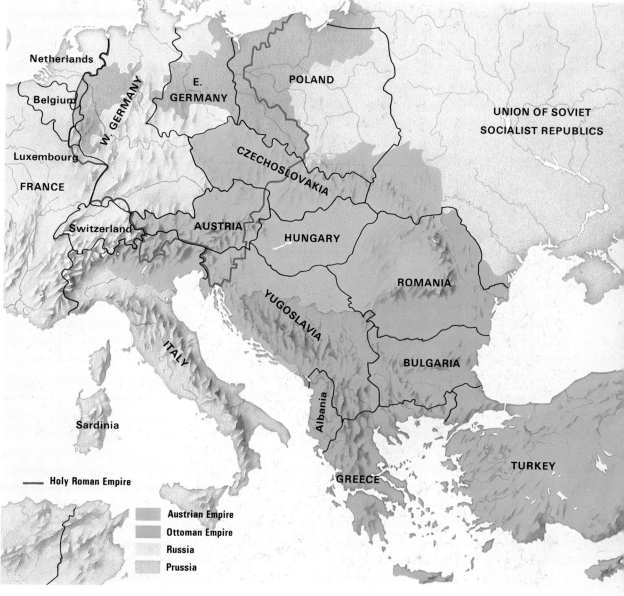

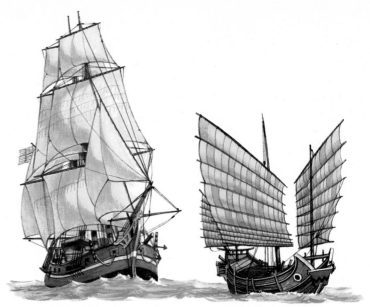

Above: A British sailing ship of the kind known as an East Indiaman, and a Chinese sailing junk. The British traded all over the Far East but the Chinese were not interested in foreign trade.

Opening Up the East

By the late 1800s the British ruled India, Burma, and Malaya. The Dutch ruled the East Indies, and the Philippines were ruled by Spain. In the north, Russia had steadily taken over the mainland until its empire reached right across to the Pacific Ocean, and in 1858 France began to build a new empire, conquering Annam, Tongking, Cambodia, and Laos.

There were two nations in the Far East which did not become part of any European empire. These were Japan and China. Neither was impressed by what they saw of the first Europeans (see page 49), and after a little while they closed their countries against them. People who had become Christians were tortured or killed. This stopped the Chinese and Japanese from following any of the great changes in industry and learning any of the new skills that people in Europe had developed.

Learning from the West

In 1853 the Americans sailed into the port of Edo near Tokyo in Japan. Two of their ships were driven by the new steam engines. The Japanese realized that they could not possibly win a sea battle against these powerful ships. The Americans made the Japanese government agree to more trading with the West. Then the young Prince Meiji became emperor. He wanted his people to copy the things that made the West powerful. Western advisers were brought in to bring the army and navy up to date. Industries and factories like Western ones were built, and soon railways were opened. Many Japanese people even began to wear Western clothes.

Japan was now so strong that it wanted to build up an empire. First it won a war against China. Then it turned against Russia, and to everyone's surprise won battles on land and sank the Russian fleet. It took over Russian-controlled land on the mainland of China. Next Japan took over Korea and in the 1930s it invaded China. Soon it controlled China's main ports. In the Second World War the Japanese conquered an enormous empire. They quickly seized Malaya and Hong Kong from the British, the East Indies from the Dutch, and Indochina from the French. They even attacked the Americans on the Pacific island of Hawaii. Japan was defeated after a few years and lost all its overseas lands.

Since the War the Japanese have worked hard and now their country is one of the world's greatest industrial nations. Japanese goods like cars, radios and televisions, and cameras are sold all over the world, and Japan is the leading builder of ships. In not much over a hundred years, it has overtaken many countries of the West.

Changes in China

The Chinese allowed Westerners to trade with them only through the ports of Canton and Macao. They considered Westerners barbarians, but they sold them silk, spices, porcelain, jade, lacquer, and tea in exchange for gold or silver. They said they did not want anything Europe could make.

Then the British discovered that the Chinese would buy opium, a drug from India. The Chinese emperor tried to stop the opium trade and war broke out. The Chinese could not win against the British steamships. More and more ports were allowed to trade with foreigners, and British ships sailed up and down China's great rivers. A British prime minister even suggested that China should be divided up into 'areas of influence' by the most powerful European states. It looked as though China might be divided up, just as Africa was (see page 71). But the Europeans could not agree which area each should take, and when rebellious Chinese besieged Europeans in Peking they realized how difficult it would be to rule China.

Little by little, the Chinese learnt some Western ways. But many of them felt changes should come more quickly. In 1911 they overthrew the emperor and set up a republic. It began to make changes. But this was difficult in a country as vast as China, and it was easily invaded by the Japanese with its Western ways. Meanwhile, a Communist Party was growing up and in 1949 it seized power. Since then, the Chinese people have been working to change centuries-old patterns of life and build up a new state that is modern in its ways and Communist in its beliefs, but that still keeps its Chinese character.

British troops seize the Chinese town of Chinkiang in 1842. This picture was painted by a British naval captain who was there at the time. The Chinese emperor had tried to stop the British from selling opium in China, and this led to war breaking out.

Once the Japanese let Europeans into their country, they soon took up Western ideas. This picture shows a group of Japanese people in Western dress. They are playing Western musical instruments and seem to be singing a Western song. In the 1880s important Japanese people could go to a government-run club to meet foreigners at balls and other events. But in 1888 a new feeling of nationalism swept through Japan. People began to want to keep up the old Japanese ways and went back to wearing their traditional dress. In 1890 the club was closed.

Opening Up Africa

Africa was the last great continent to be explored by the Europeans. They knew its coasts, but they were put off the interior by the climate, the threat of diseases that killed early travellers, and the difficulty of moving far inland. The goods they wanted, such as slaves, gold, ivory, and timber, were brought by the Africans themselves to the European trading stations built along the coasts.

North Africa became part of the Muslim empire in the early Middle Ages, and the Arabs built many ports on the south-east coasts. Arab traders travelled south across the Sahara Desert to the great medieval kingdoms of Ancient Ghana and Mali, and later to the Songhai empire on the river Niger. The Arabs have described the rich and powerful cities there. But we know little about the rest of Africa before the Europeans arrived there. The Africans did not develop a written language, so there are no records of their history.

The First Colonies

The first Europeans to settle in Africa were the Portuguese. In the 1400s and 1500s they built trading posts down the west coast, and at Mozambique on the east coast. They were followed by the Dutch, who founded a colony at the Cape of Good Hope. Dutch ships stopped here on their way to the East, and stocked up with fresh fruit and vegetables grown by Dutch farmers. Portuguese, Dutch, British, and

This bronze group was made in the forest kingdom of Benin, in west Africa. It is very difficult to date it, since the work of Benin craftsmen changed little for hundreds of years after the 1400s. It shows a king, or *oba*, and two attendants.

Dr Livingstone arrives at Lake Ngami in 1849. Livingstone went to Africa as a missionary and soon travelled farther and farther into unknown parts of the continent. He made many friends among the Africans. He hoped to open up trade routes into Africa, which he thought would cut down the slave trade. During his travels he explored the rivers Zambezi and Congo and discovered the Victoria Falls and Lake Nyasa.

French all took part in the terrible slave trade from the west coast. Over 10 million Africans were taken to America and the West Indies to work on the cotton, sugar, and rice plantations there, before the slave trade was stopped in the early 1800s.

Europeans Take Over

In 1788 the Association for Promoting the Discovery of the Interior Parts of Africa was set up in London. It began to send expeditions to explore the continent. Many of the first explorers died of fever and some of them disappeared. But by the 1870s the great rivers of Africa had been explored. European countries decided to set up colonies there. It looked as though war might break out between them, but they managed to settle their quarrels and divided the continent between themselves.

The Africans could do little about this. The Europeans were armed with guns and could easily defeat them. Many African chiefs signed treaties handing over their lands to Europeans, but they did

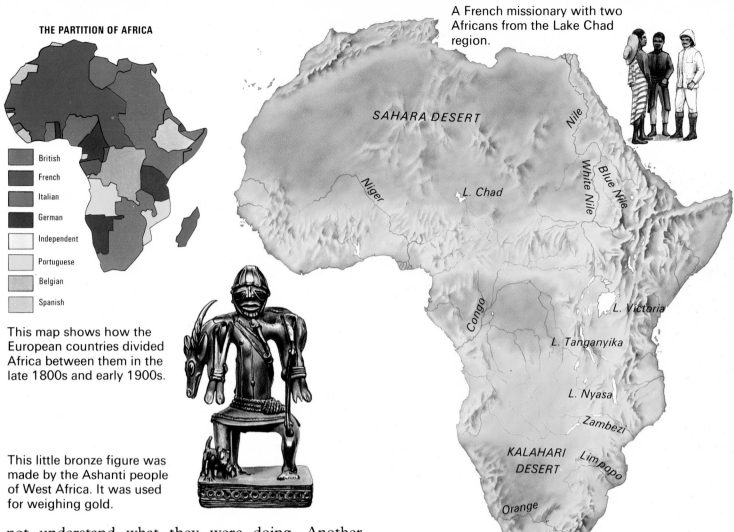

THE PARTITION OF AFRICA

- British
- French
- Italian
- German
- Independent
- Portuguese
- Belgian
- Spanish

This map shows how the European countries divided Africa between them in the late 1800s and early 1900s.

This little bronze figure was made by the Ashanti people of West Africa. It was used for weighing gold.

A French missionary with two Africans from the Lake Chad region.

SAHARA DESERT
Niger
Nile
White Nile
Blue Nile
L. Chad
Congo
L. Victoria
L. Tanganyika
L. Nyasa
Zambezi
KALAHARI DESERT
Limpopo
Orange
Cape of Good Hope

not understand what they were doing. Another problem was that the Europeans did not take the African peoples into account when they were dividing Africa up into colonies. People of one tribe might find that some of their lands were part of a French colony, while the rest were ruled by the British. In other places, peoples who were old enemies found themselves in the same new country.

In many parts of Africa Europeans farmed or cultivated the land. They planted crops like sugar cane, ground nuts, and coffee. They found out what kinds of cattle would do well there. They sent timber and ivory back to Europe, and mined for gold, diamonds, and copper. Some of the Europeans were good rulers, and did their best to bring law and order. They helped to stop local wars and to control human and animal diseases. They set up schools and hospitals, and built roads and railways. But in some of the colonies the Europeans proved cruel masters, who thought only about the money to be made.

The last British colony in Africa to become independent was Zimbabwe, formerly Rhodesia. The white settlers there refused to give up control of the country to the Africans. Instead they declared their country independent in 1965, without the agreement of Britain or the Africans. The Africans fought a guerilla war until 1979 when Britain arranged a settlement, and Zimbabwe became independent in 1980. Here British and African leaders sign their agreement.

The European rule of Africa lasted less than a hundred years. After the Second World War, almost all the countries became independent. But in that short time many Africans had learned European ways of life and government, and are following them still. In the south of the continent one huge white-ruled country remains. This is the Republic of South Africa, which grew up from the first Dutch settlement. The white people there refuse to share government with the Africans.

New Communications

In ancient times people **travelled on foot**, with their goods loaded on pack animals such as camels, asses, and horses. They covered about 5 kilometres (3 miles) an hour.

A **stage coach** could travel at about 15 kilometres (9 miles) an hour along reasonable roads.

During the 1800s and 1900s many new ways of travel have been developed, and old ones improved. As a result, it has become very much quicker, easier, and cheaper to travel from one place to another. Today barriers like deserts and mountain ranges are easily crossed by roads and railways. We can fly from one side of the world to the other in less than a day – a journey that would have taken several months by sailing ship. Public transport systems including railways, ships, aircraft, and buses carry large numbers, while many people own their own cars.

PACIFIC OCEAN

Sacramento
St Joseph
New York
NORTH AMERICA
Mississippi
•Los Angeles

The **Romans** built good **roads** all over their Empire, from Britain to the river Euphrates. Roman soldiers marched 48 kilometres (30 miles) in a day, for days at a time, carrying their equipment.

Britain
London
EUROPE

ATLANTIC OCEAN

In 1838 the **steamship** *Great Western* sailed from Bristol to New York in $15\frac{1}{2}$ days. A hundred years later, the *Queen Mary*, a huge and luxurious passenger **liner**, made the Atlantic crossing in just under four days, at an average speed of 31.9 knots. Today the journey from London to New York takes three hours by supersonic **plane**.

AFRICA

Crossing America. In the 1860s the journey by stage coach from St Joseph in Missouri to Sacramento in California, a distance of 3164 kilometres (1966 miles) took three weeks. Even the 'Pony Express' mail took 10 days. By 1900 a train from New York to Los Angeles, nearly twice as far, took four days. Today the same journey takes 7 hours by air.

CENTRAL AMERICA

Panama Canal

The **Panama Canal** was opened in 1914. Now people no longer had to sail round South America to travel from the Atlantic Ocean to the Pacific Ocean.

Right: The *Spirit of St Louis*, in which Charles Lindbergh made the first solo transatlantic flight in 1927. Below: The supersonic *Concorde*.

Amazon

SOUTH AMERICA

The first **railway** on which all trains were drawn by steam engines was opened in 1830. It ran between Liverpool and Manchester in northern England. A train could travel along it at over 57 kilometres (36 miles) an hour. Today passenger trains travel at over 200 kilometres (125 miles) an hour.

The first non-stop **flight** across the Atlantic was made in 1919 by Alcock and Brown. It took them 16 hours 27 minutes to fly from Newfoundland to Ireland.

These new transport systems carry goods and letters as well as people, and airmail posts take only a few days. But new inventions make instant communication possible all over the world. They include the telephone and radio, and machines by which a message typed in one place is received thousands of kilometres away only seconds later. Today what happens in one country is known all over the world the same day, and such news is spread by papers and by radio and television programmes. People today know more about the world than ever before.

The fastest ever sailing ships were the **clippers**. They were first built in the mid 1800s. They carried tea from China and India and wool from Australia back to Europe. They could sail at more than 20 knots. Sometimes the clippers used to race one another. In 1866 two clippers set out from Foochow in China. They sailed 25,750 kilometres (16,000 miles) to London in 99 days, and arrived only 20 minutes apart.

UNION OF SOVIET SOCIALIST REPUBLICS

Moscow

Vladivostock

Lydia

Euphrates

Susa

Suez Canal

Nile

CHINA

Foochow

INDIA

The **Trans-Siberian Railway** links Moscow and Vladivostok. Work on it began in 1891. It covers just under 9500 kilometres (5900 miles) and the journey takes eight days.

PACIFIC OCEAN

Today an ordinary **car** or **truck** can easily average 65 kilometres (45 miles) an hour.

The Persian **Royal Road** ran from Susa to Lydia in Anatolia, more than 2400 kilometres (1500 miles) away. Royal messengers travelled from end to end in only nine days. Normally such a distance would have taken about three months.

INDIAN OCEAN

The English **merchant ships** known as East Indiamen sailed around the Far East in the 1700s and 1800s. Their greatest speed was about 9 knots. (A knot is the measurement of speed at sea. It is 1.9 kilometres, or 1.2 miles, an hour.)

The **Suez Canal** was built in the 1860s. It cut the journey from Europe to India by thousands of kilometres; before, ships had had to sail round Africa.

NEW ZEALAND

73

The World Today

The last two hundred years have seen more new inventions and changes in people's lives than at any other time in history. All sorts of machines have been invented which make things quickly and cheaply and carry out jobs easily. Manmade materials make clothes that are cheap, warm, and easy to look after. New medicines have been discovered which mean that many people live much longer, healthier lives.

These inventions and discoveries soon spread through the richer countries of the world, and life there became safer and easier. More people than ever before learnt to read and write. At the same time, new, fast ways of travel such as railways, cars, and later aircraft made it quick and easy for people to go from one part of the world to another. Inventions like the telephone and radio allowed them to talk to people in other countries.

All these changes meant that happenings in one part of the world quickly affected far distant places. In two terrible world wars, millions of people were killed with new, deadly weapons. Since then, people have begun to realize that they must work together to prevent such appalling wars ever happening again. Some 150 countries have joined together to form the United Nations. They meet together to talk over problems, and though they have not prevented wars altogether, they have helped to stop some, and have brought others to an end. The United Nations does not just try to prevent wars. Its members work together to bring better health to poor countries, to help them grow more food, and to teach their people to read and write, and how to use and make machines.

There are other ways, too, in which countries help one another. When there is a great disaster like an earthquake or a flood, help comes from all over the world. And richer countries give money to help poorer ones.

There are many very serious problems for the world today. The most powerful countries have many quarrels, and if war broke out between them millions of people would be killed by the deadlier and deadlier weapons they are making. It looks as though the coal and oil which we use for fuel may run out before very long. It even looks as though there may be so many people living in the world that they cannot all be fed. But the great hope is that people from all different countries are working together to try to make the future safer and better for everyone.

Workers digging an irrigation channel in Indonesia. It is part of a project run by the Food and Agricultural Organization, an agency of the United Nations which works to help people feed themselves.

IMPORTANT DATES

1914   The First World War broke out between Germany, Austria-Hungary, Bulgaria, and the Ottoman Empire on one side and Belgium, Britain and its Empire, France, Italy, Japan, Russia, Serbia, and (later) the United States on the other. It ended with the defeat of Germany and its allies (the Central Powers) in 1918.

1917   The Russians revolted against their ruler, the Tsar, who abdicated. Later he and his family were killed. At first there was a moderate government, but after a few months Communists seized power. A civil war followed and eventually the Communists ruled the whole country.

1923   Turkey became a republic under Mustapha Kemal.

1929   The United States' stock market suddenly collapsed as people sold millions of shares in a panic. This was followed by a time of economic troubles and unemployment in many parts of the world, known as the Great Depression.

1933   Adolf Hitler, leader of the Nazi Party, became chancellor (chief minister) of Germany.

1936   Civil war broke out in Spain between the Republican government and right-wing Nationalists under General Franco, who won in 1939 with German and Italian help.

1939   Germany invaded Poland on September 1st and the Second World War broke out. Germany and its allies, which included Italy and Japan, fought Britain, France, the United States and their allies, who won in 1945.

1945   The United Nations Organization was set up; 51 countries signed its charter and many more have since joined it.

1950   War broke out in Korea between the Communist, Russian-backed North, and the South which had United Nations

Above: A Norwegian soldier, part of a United Nations peace-keeping force in the Lebanon. Forces like these act rather like policemen, trying to stop fighting in troubled areas. Below: A child in a refugee camp gets food from a Red Cross centre. The Red Cross, known in Muslim countries as the Red Crescent, is an international organization that does a great deal to help refugees and people suffering from disasters like earthquakes, floods, and famines.

	help. Peace was made in 1953, with the frontier as it had been before the war.
1956	The Egyptians took control of the Suez Canal from the British and French. Israel invaded Egypt after many skirmishes on the border. Britain and France attacked Egypt, but withdrew after pressure from the United Nations.
1957	The first Russian satellite was launched and the Space Age began. The first manned space flight was that of the Russian Yuri Gagarin in 1961, while the Americans put the first men on the Moon in 1969. War in Vietnam between the Communist North and American-backed South lasted from now until 1975, when Vietnam was united as a Communist country after the Americans withdrew.
1963	President John F. Kennedy of the United States was assassinated.
1967	War broke out between Israel and Egypt. Israel captured Arab-held Jerusalem and much Egyptian land. Civil war broke out in Nigeria when its eastern region tried unsuccessfully to break away.
1973	In the Yom Kippur War between Israel and the Egyptians and Syrians, both sides gained some land but lost some. Arab positions were strengthened.
1979	The Shah of Iran was deposed and an Islamic Republic set up.
1980	Britain's last colony in Africa became independent as Zimbabwe.
1981	President Sadat of Egypt, who was unpopular with many Arabs because of his efforts to make peace with Israel, was assassinated.

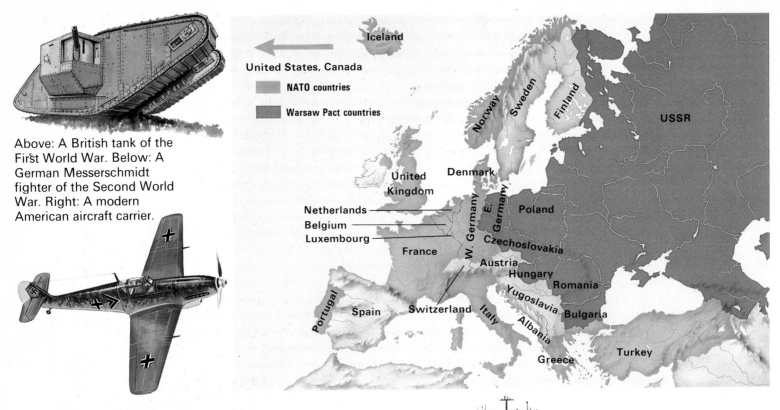

Above: A British tank of the First World War. Below: A German Messerschmidt fighter of the Second World War. Right: A modern American aircraft carrier.

Iceland

United States, Canada

NATO countries

Warsaw Pact countries

USSR

Norway
Sweden
Finland

Denmark

United Kingdom

Netherlands
Belgium
Luxembourg

W. Germany
E. Germany
Poland
Czechoslovakia
France
Austria
Hungary
Romania
Switzerland
Italy
Yugoslavia
Bulgaria
Albania
Portugal
Spain
Greece
Turkey

The World at War

The 1900s have seen a number of terrible wars. Two of them are known as world wars, for though they started in Europe countries from all over the world joined in. Others have been smaller. There have been civil wars within countries, when people have tried to overthrow a government they disagreed with, and there have been fights between people of different beliefs. These wars have been made even more awful by the new weapons which people have developed.

The First World War lasted from 1914 to 1918, and the Second from 1939 to 1945. The First War was caused by rivalries between nations in Europe, who feared that one country might get too powerful. They made alliances with one another, so that when one country was threatened, others were drawn in to defend it. Most of the great battles of this war took place in Europe, where a great line of trenches and barbed wire stretched from the Belgian coast to the Alps, with Germany and its allies on one side, and France, Britain, and their allies on the other. Hundreds of thousands of men died in gaining just a few metres of ground for their side. By the end of the war tanks and planes were coming into use, so when the Second Word War came, it was fought in a different way. Now Britain, France, Russia and their allies were fighting to prevent the Nazi Germans and Fascist Italians controlling Europe. Planes, tanks, and motor transport swept swiftly into action, often covering great distances in a few days. This war spread to the Far East when the Japanese attacked

The map above shows the countries of the North Atlantic Treaty Organization (which also includes the United States of America and Canada) and of the Communist Warsaw Pact countries. Since the Second World War these two groups have opposed each other in what is called the 'Cold War'.

America and invaded British, French, and Dutch colonies.

In the First World War ordinary people at home had a hard time, but soldiers fought under the most appalling conditions and millions were killed. The Second World War was even worse for the men, women, and children at home. Submarines prowled under the oceans, sinking ships carrying food, so strict food rationing was imposed. Both sides bombed each other's cities, and many civilians were killed and factories, homes, and offices destroyed.

The 'Cold War'

In the Second War the Russians fought on the side of the British and Americans. But after the war, their alliance broke up. Russia set up Communist governments in the countries of eastern Europe, which it had taken over from the Germans at the end of the war. The Americans were afraid that the Russians were preparing to invade the non-Communist countries of western Europe. The Russians thought that the Americans wanted to control Europe. The rivalry between these two great countries is known as the 'Cold War'. It is not a war in the true sense, since they have not fought each other, but there have been several occasions when war has nearly broken out between them. Both have built up groups of allies. Today, people often talk about Western countries, meaning America and its allies, and Eastern countries meaning Russia and the countries it controls. Both groups try to win the newly independent countries of Africa and Asia to their side, but some countries want to remain independent of East and West alike.

After the Second World War the Communists took over power in China and several other Far Eastern countries. The Americans tried to stop Communism spreading. They and their allies prevented the Communists from North Korea from taking over South Korea. Later the Americans fought a bitter war against Communism in Vietnam, but they withdrew and Vietnam and its neighbours are now under Communist rule.

Nuclear Power

At the end of the Second World War the Americans dropped a new and terrible kind of bomb on Japan. This was the first nuclear bomb, and it was far more destructive than any bomb known before. Since then, all the most powerful countries have armed themselves with nuclear bombs. But they know that if one country drops such a bomb others will follow, and many millions of people would be killed. So far no one has dared do so.

Above: American troops man an anti-tank gun during the Second World War. The United States of America delayed joining in both world wars, but in both cases it played a decisive part in winning them. Below: Vietnamese refugees run for a helicopter to take them to safety. This century has seen millions of people made homeless by wars, and forced to move from the country where they were born.

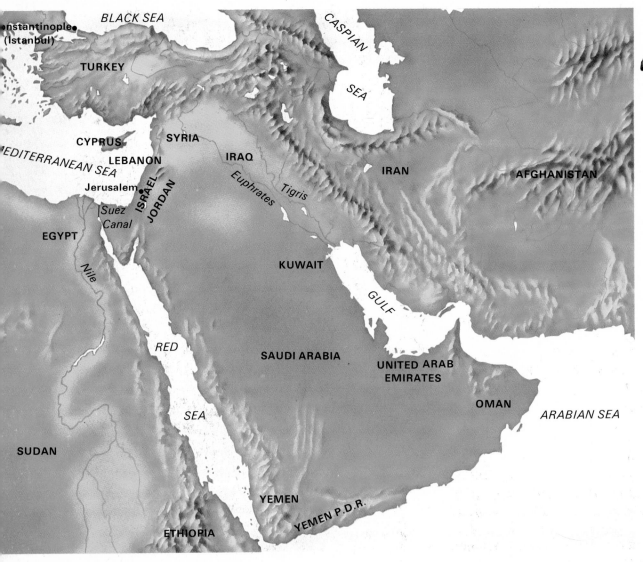

Above: This statue shows the Turkish leader Mustapha Kemal. He is also called Ataturk, which means 'father of the Turks'. He became president of Turkey after the First World War, when the Ottoman Empire finally broke up. Life in Turkey had hardly changed for hundreds of years under the Ottomans, and Mustapha Kemal did all he could to bring his country up to date.

The Near East

The discovery of oil in the Near East has brought great wealth but many people still live in their traditional way. Here a shepherd guides his flock while oil wells flare in the background.

The Near East lies where the continents of Europe, Africa, and Asia meet, and much of the trade between East and West has had to pass through its frontiers. As a result, what happens there has always been very important to the great trading nations of the world. Much of the area is desert. Little rain falls there, and what farming there is depends on irrigation. Two of the world's greatest civilizations grew up there – in Egypt and in Mesopotamia, which is now called Iraq – but for much of their history the desert countries of the Near East have been very poor.

The Fall of the Ottomans

For hundreds of years most of the Near East was part of the great Ottoman Empire. The people there were almost all Muslims, and they spoke Arabic. Then the Ottoman Empire lost its power. Egypt came under British and French control; it became especially important when the Suez Canal was built to link the Mediterranean Sea with the Red Sea and through it

the Indian Ocean. This made it far quicker to sail to India and the Far East, and ships of all nations steamed through it. After the First World War the Ottoman Empire broke up. The Turks ruled only over Turkey and a tiny part of Europe, including the Turkish capital Constantinople. Some Ottoman lands in the Near East were handed to France and Britain to look after until they became ready to rule themselves.

Jews and Muslims

Another thing that makes the Near East important to other countries is that it was the birthplace of three of the world's greatest religions – Judaism, Christianity, and Islam. Jerusalem is a holy city for people of all three faiths. The area known until recently as Palestine, running along the east coast of the Mediterranean, was the home of the Jews until most of them were driven out by the Romans.

In 1917 it was suggested that a Jewish 'homeland' should be set up in the area, where Jews from all over the world could come and settle. This did not please the Muslims who had lived there for hundreds of years. At first only a few Jews arrived, but after the Second World War hundreds of thousands of Jews flooded into the area. In the fighting that followed the state of Israel was set up, and many Palestinians fled to the neighbouring Arab countries. There they still live as refugees; they want to go back to their old home, and not to settle in the lands that have given them shelter. Some of them attack Israel to try to win their homes back. They are given support by other Muslims, and since the new state of Israel was born there have been three wars and a great deal of other fighting.

In the last few years many Muslims in the Near East have begun to think people are taking up Western ways too fast, and are forgetting the teachings of the Koran. In 1979 a religious leader called the Ayatollah Khomeini led a revolution in Iran, which sent its ruler the Shah into exile and set up a new religious state. Here a crowd of Iranians wave banners showing portraits of the Ayatollah.

Riches from Oil

For almost all their history, countries of the Near East such as Saudi-Arabia and Kuwait have been some of the poorest in the world. But in the 20th century oil has been found there. Now they are almost unbelievably rich. They can give their people free education and free medicine, and they buy enormous quantities of goods from the Western countries. They also give a great deal of aid to poorer countries. They can bargain with the industrial countries of the West and with Japan over the price of their oil, and they can threaten to cut off supplies. This makes them very powerful. But a feeling has grown up recently among some Muslims that they have been accepting too many Western ways too fast. They believe that the new ways of living do not fit in with their religion. Some of them say that religion should play a much bigger part in their government, and in Iran this led to the taking over of control by a religious leader, the Ayatollah Khomeini.

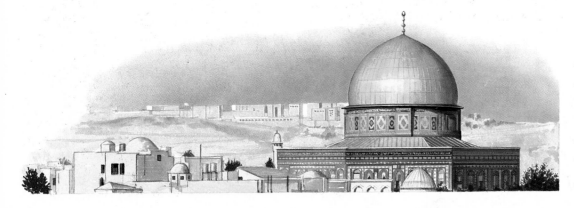

The mosque called the Dome of the Rock in Jerusalem. This is a holy city for Jews, Christians, and Muslims, who have fought over it often in the past. Now it is part of the Jewish state of Israel. The Muslim Arabs bitterly resent this.

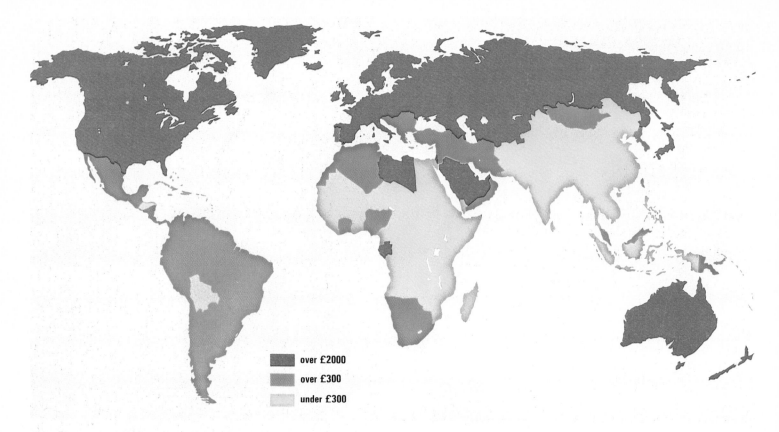

over £2000

over £300

under £300

Rich and Poor

In the 1700s and 1800s, several European countries built up large empires scattered over many parts of the world. Today these empires have largely disappeared. Since the Second World War, most of the colonies have gained their independence. Those that are left are small areas which elect their own ruling council or parliament to look after home affairs, while the colonial power looks after defence and foreign affairs.

Gaining Independence

There were many problems as countries gained their independence. Often the European rulers did not want to allow their colonies to rule themselves, and in some places there were years of fighting between the colonial soldiers and independence fighters. European settlers who had lived in the colonies for several generations did not want to hand back their land. They refused to share the government with the people of the country and this too sometimes led to war. In many countries, there were few people who had any practice in government, and this made it difficult for them to run their countries by themselves.

Many countries have had a difficult time since independence. Sometimes the people who led them to independence proved bad rulers. Several of the newly independent countries have had rebellions, and in some of them dictators have taken over. In some countries, too, terrible civil wars have taken place between different tribes which had long been enemies

This map shows the average income of people living in the world today. In some ways it is misleading, since the figures are worked out country by country; and in some nations a few people are very rich while most people are quite poor. But it does show the general difference between the wealthy industrial countries, and the poorer developing countries of Africa and Asia.

but which had been brought together into the same country by the Europeans.

In India there was great trouble between the Hindus and the Muslims. Neither was willing to be ruled by the other. It was decided to split the country into Hindu India, and Muslim Pakistan in the north-east and north-west. Many Hindus and Muslims left their homes to move to regions ruled by people of their own faith, and there were terrible massacres in which hundreds of thousands of people were killed.

Most of the countries of the British Empire have stayed linked together as members of the Commonwealth of Nations. They still all share the leadership of the British Queen. Other newly independent countries have also kept close links with the former colonial powers, who help to train their people in modern skills and who give them aid. One tie is language. People in a colony often learnt the language of their rulers. This makes it easy for them to deal with one another.

Rich and Poor

Most of the former colonies are in Africa, Asia, and the West Indies. If you look at the map at the top of this page, you can see that the people in these parts of the world are much poorer than those of most of

Europe and the USSR, the United States and Canada, South Africa, Japan, Australia, and New Zealand. These poorer countries are often called the developing countries; the others are developed countries.

People in developing countries have many problems. Food is often in short supply, and there are few schools, doctors, and hospitals. They can expect to live perhaps only half as long as the people in developed nations. These countries do not have many industries and most of their people are farmers, who can grow just enough to feed their families. If droughts, floods, or pests destroy the crops, there are famines when thousands of people may die of starvation. Despite this, the populations of the developing countries are growing much faster than those of the developed countries.

In rich countries people can easily buy things from all different parts of the world. This supermarket dairy counter is typical of large shops. It contains butter, cheese, and cooked meat from nine or ten different countries.

In many parts of the world people are still very poor. They can barely get enough to eat and live in very simple houses. They have to walk a long way to the nearest source of water, which has to be carried back to their village. This photograph shows a village in a poor area of Nigeria.

Glossary

Acropolis The highest point of an Ancient Greek city. It was both a citadel with strong defensive walls, and a sacred enclosure containing the chief temples of the city.

Ally A partner in peace or war.

Amphitheatre An open-air theatre with rising tiers of seats arranged around a central stage.

Annex To take possession of land or a country, usually without having any rights to it.

Aqueduct Structure for carrying a water supply.

Archaeology The study of peoples of the past through their objects and ruins that still survive.

Artillery Guns mounted on wheels.

Assassinate To murder someone, especially a political or religious leader, for political purposes.

Barbarians People living outside the borders of a developed society with a strong culture and way of life were often regarded by those inside as barbarians.

Boers Dutch colonists in South Africa, and their descendants.

Bronze An alloy (mixture) of copper and tin. It is much harder than pure copper and was first discovered about 3000 BC.

Caravan A group of merchants or pilgrims travelling together, usually for safety.

Catholic Church The Christian Church headed by the Pope in Rome.

Citadel The fortified strongpoint of a city, often on a hill.

City state A city which ruled itself and the farmland around it.

Civil war War between groups of citizens of the same country.

Colonize To found settlements abroad which are ruled on behalf of the home country.

Colony A group of people living in a new country, but keeping ties with their home country.

Communists Members of a political party which believes that all property and means of production should belong to the State.

Conquistador The Spanish word for 'conqueror'. It is the name given to the Spanish adventurers who went to South America in search of treasure.

Convoy A number of ships or land vehicles which travel together for one another's protection.

Cuneiform A writing system formed by wedge shapes, developed in Mesopotamia and widely used in the Near East in ancient times.

Democracy From Greek words meaning rule by the people. Usually, this means that a government is elected for fixed periods by the citizens of a State.

Dictator An absolute ruler who allows no opposition to his power.

Dominion A self-governing territory. A Dominion within the British Empire was a self-governing territory that recognized the British Crown.

Dynasty A series of rulers from the same family.

EEC European Economic Community (the Common Market).

Emigrate To leave the country of which you are a citizen to settle in another country.

Excavation The unearthing of an historic site.

Excommunication A punishment issued by the Pope which took away the right of a member of the Roman Catholic Church to the services of the Church, including forgiveness of sins and a Catholic burial. If a ruler was excommunicated, his subjects were often excommunicated as well.

Expedition A journey taken for a special purpose.

Export To send raw materials or goods from the country in which they were produced for sale in another country.

Fascism The political theory that believes that the rights of individuals should take second place to the interests of the State.

Federation A group of states joined together for defence and government.

Feudalism A system where a great lord or ruler owns the land, which he grants to lesser lords or peasants in return for services, usually military or work on the land.

Flood plain The area around a river which is affected when the river floods. The silt laid down by the flood usually makes the soil very fertile.

Great Britain The name given to the kingdoms of Scotland and England after their Union in 1707.

Great Wall A huge defence system, some 2400 kilometres (1500 miles) long, built by the Chinese during the Ch'in dynasty. It was built of earth and stone, and much of it remains today.

Guerilla A member of an irregular military force which is usually split into small independent groups.

Hieroglyphics Writing which used picture symbols which sometimes represented words, sometimes consonants.

Horde A large tribe or troop of nomadic warriors.

Imperialism The rule of one people by another and the belief that a strong nation has a right and a duty to govern weaker nations.

Import To bring raw materials or goods into a country which have been produced in another country.

Islam The religion which holds that Allah is the only God and Muhammad is his prophet. Islam also means the culture and way of life established by Muhammad's followers.

Jews The name given to those Israelites who returned to Jerusalem and its neighbourhood after their exile to Babylon in the 500s BC.

Lapis lazuli A semi-precious blue stone which was greatly valued by people long ago and used by them for decoration.

Legends Religious and historical stories which have been handed down from generation to generation.

Liberal Any political movement which favours freedom from central control and is against privilege.

Loyalist Someone whose sympathies and allegiance remain with the sovereign or home country.

Manuscript A hand-written document or book.

Medieval The word used to describe something which is connected with the Middle Ages.

Migration The movement of a body of people or animals from one area to another.

Missionaries People sent to make new converts to a religion, particularly in other countries.

Moors The name given to the Muslims living in North Africa who conquered Spain in the 700s.

Mosaic A picture or design produced by piecing together tiny pieces of glass and stone.

Muslim A follower of Islam.

NATO The North Atlantic Treaty Organization.

Navigation The art or practice of steering a particular course and the skills that enable the course to be held.

Near East The general name given to the countries of western Asia, stretching from the Dardanelles to the Arabian peninsula. The term sometimes includes Egypt.

Netherlands Until 1609, the name for the area which is now Belgium and the Kingdom of the Netherlands (Holland). At that time the northern part, the United Provinces or Holland, gained independence; the southern part (modern Belgium) was called the Spanish Netherlands. Today only Holland is called the Netherlands.

Nomads People who move with their flocks and herds in search of grazing land. Many nomads move only between summer and winter pastures.

Opium A powerful drug produced from the seeds of a certain type of poppy.

Papyrus Paper made from layers of papyrus reeds.

Parchment A thin piece of goat- or sheepskin used for writing on.

Patriot Someone who loves his or her country and who may be willing to fight for its freedom.

Plague A disease which spreads rapidly killing large numbers of people. In the Middle Ages the most dreaded was bubonic plague (the Black Death) which was carried by rat fleas.

Plantation A large estate growing one type of plant, looked after by workers living on the land under the direction of the owner.

Proclamation An official public announcement.

Protestants Christians who followed Luther in breaking away from the Roman Catholic Church, after trying to change practices to which they objected.

Raw materials Natural substances, such as coal, wood, rubber, and cotton, which are processed by industry to produce other goods.

Reformation The movement begun by Luther to reform the Roman Catholic Church. Luther particularly objected to the sale of forgiveness of sins by the Church.

Refugees Someone who is forced to leave his home by enemy or political action or by a natural disaster, and seek safety elsewhere.

Scurvy A disease from which sailors on long sea voyages suffered, due to a lack of vitamin C usually found in fresh fruit and vegetables.

Seal A carved stone stamped with a distinctive design for signing or sealing documents.

Shrine A holy place, usually on a site where some important event connected with a religion took place, or where relics are kept.

Smelting Releasing iron from its ore by heating the ore in a furnace.

Spice Islands The name given to the islands of South-East Asia from which spices were exported to Europe.

Steppes The high, cold plains of Russia and Central Asia.

Technology The practical use of scientific ideas.

Telegraph A machine for sending messages or signals by electrical impulses along wires.

Terracotta Clay which has been shaped and baked. It is often painted and glazed for decoration and to make it waterproof.

Tributary A stream that feeds into a larger stream or river. It is also the name given to a state which makes payments (tribute) to a more powerful state.

Tribute Money or goods paid by one person or state to another more powerful one. The payment was to acknowledge the other's higher authority or was in return for peace and protection.

Tsar The Russian form of the word 'caesar', used for the ruler.

Vassal state A state separate from, but ruled by, a more powerful one.

Warsaw Pact An alliance set up after the Second World War between the USSR and most of the countries of Eastern Europe.

Map: The World Today

Greenland

ICELAND

CANADA

UNITED STATES
OF AMERICA

IRELAND

UNITE
KINGD

FRA

SPAIN

PORTUGAL

MOROCCO

ALG

MA

WESTERN
SAHARA

MAURITANIA

TROPIC OF CANCER

MEXICO

BAHAMAS

CUBA

46

53

54 55

56

CAPE
VERDE
ISLANDS

26

27

28

29

32

48

50

47

52

57

VENEZUELA

58 5960

30

31

IVORY COAST

49

51

COLOMBIA

EQUATOR

ECUADOR

PERU

BRAZIL

BOLIVIA

TROPIC OF CAPRICORN

PARAGUAY

URUGUAY

CHILE

ARGENTINA

Falkland Islands

1 DENMARK	11 YUGOSLAVIA
2 NETHERLANDS	12 ALBANIA
3 BELGIUM	13 CYPRUS
4 LUXEMBOURG	14 LEBANON
5 W. GERMANY	15 ISRAEL
6 E. GERMANY	16 SYRIA
7 SWITZERLAND	17 JORDAN
8 AUSTRIA	18 KUWAIT
9 CZECHOSLOVAKIA	19 BAHRAIN
10 HUNGARY	20 UNITED ARAB EMIRATES

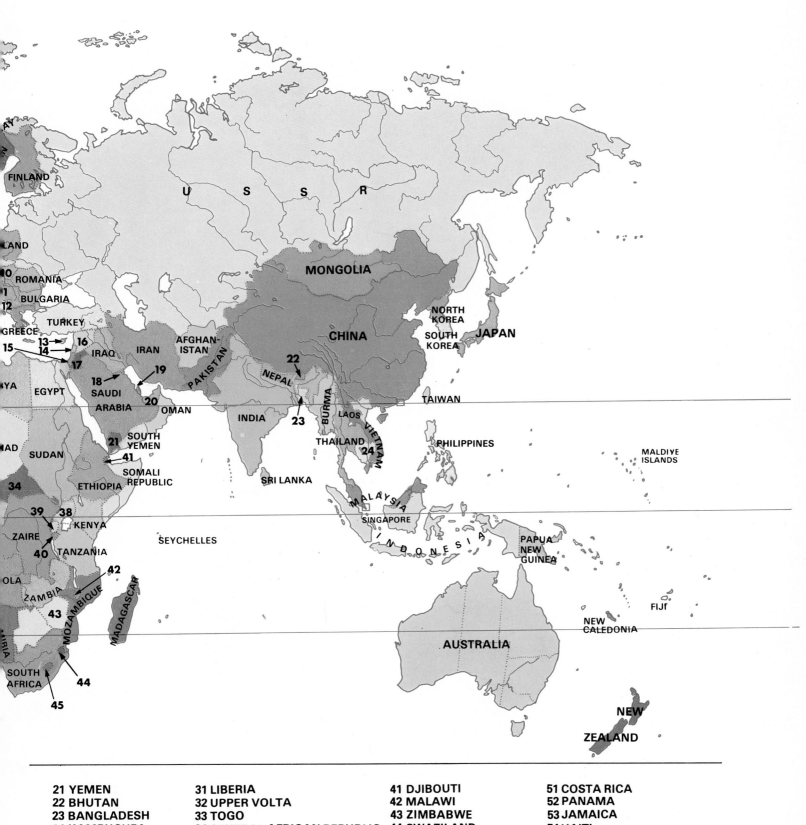

21 YEMEN	31 LIBERIA	41 DJIBOUTI	51 COSTA RICA
22 BHUTAN	32 UPPER VOLTA	42 MALAWI	52 PANAMA
23 BANGLADESH	33 TOGO	43 ZIMBABWE	53 JAMAICA
24 KAMPUCHEA	34 CENTRAL AFRICAN REPUBLIC	44 SWAZILAND	54 HAITI
25 TUNISIA	35 EQUATORIAL GUINEA	45 LESOTHO	55 DOMINICAN REPUBLIC
26 SENEGAL	36 GABON	46 BELIZE	56 PUERTO RICO
27 GAMBIA	37 CAMEROON	47 GUATEMALA	57 TRINIDAD AND TOBAGO
28 GUINEA-BISSAU	38 UGANDA	48 HONDURAS	58 GUYANA
29 GUINEA	39 RWANDA	49 EL SALVADOR	59 SURINAM
30 SIERRA LEONE	40 BURUNDI	50 NICARAGUA	60 FRENCH GUIANA

World History

BRITAIN	EUROPE	NEAR EAST AND NORTH AFRICA	ASIA AND AMERICA
BC	**BC**	**BC**	**BC**
*c.*4000 Farming develops in Britain	*c.*6500 Farming begins in Greece and the Aegean	*c.*8000 Farming begins	*c.*6000 Rice cultivation in Far East
		*c.*4000– Invention of wheel, 3500 plough and sail in Mesopotamia and Egypt	
		*c.*3500 Early writing in Mesopotamia and Egypt	
*c.*1300 Building of hill-forts begins		*c.*2700 Age of Pyramids in *c.*2200 Egypt	*c.*2700 Harappan civilization 1750 in Indus Valley
	*c.*2000– Minoan and Mycenean 1200 civilization in Crete and Greece	*c.*2000– Hittite civilization *c.*1200 in Turkey	*c.*1750– Shang dynasty in 1000 China
	*c.*750– Greek and Phoenicians *c.*550 colonize Mediterranean and Black Sea	*c.*1200– Domination of Assyrian *c.*650 Empire	1000– Chou dynasty in *c.*500 China
	490–479 Battles of the Persian Wars	*c.*550– Achaemenid Empire in 330 Persia	
	431–404 Peloponnesian War		
	*c.*380– Work of Plato, Euclid 300 and Aristotle	334–323 Campaigns of Alexander the Great	*c.*320 Mauryan Empire in India
	*c.*327– Main period of Roman 300 expansion		*c.*200BC– Han dynasty in China *c.*AD220
	27 Octavian takes title of Augustus: end of Roman republic	*c.*6 Birth of Jesus	
AD	**AD**	**AD**	**AD**
43 Roman conquest begins		*c.*30 Crucifixion of Jesus, founder of Christianity	
61 Rebellion of Boudica		226–636 Sassanid Empire in Persia	
122 Hadrian's Wall begun	284–305 Reign of Diocletian. Empire reorganized and divided into East and West.	313 Freedom of Christian worship in Roman Empire	*c.*300– Mayan civilization in *c.*900 Central America
			304–8 Huns invade China
367 Invasion of Picts and Scots	378 Valens defeated by Visigoths at Adrianople. Germanic peoples move into Europe	429–44 Vandals occupy North Africa	*c.*320 Gupta Empire in Ganges Valley: 'Golden Age' of Hindu culture
408 Roman troops finally withdraw	410 Sack of Rome	533–4 Belisarius reconquers North Africa for Justinian	*c.*300– Main spread of 500 Buddhism in China
*c.*400– Angles, Saxons and *c.*600 Jutes migrate and settle	496 Baptism of Clovis, king of the Franks		*c.*520 Decimal system invented in India
	535–40 Justinian reconquers Italy	540 Persian-Byzantine war begins	
563 St Columba arrives at Iona	568 Lombards settle in Italy	622 Muhammad goes to Medina	618–906 T'ang dynasty in China
597 St Augustine arrives in Kent	*c.*600 Slavs move into Balkans	636–43 Arab conquest of Syria, Egypt and Persia	646 Taika reform in Japan
	711 Muslims invade Spain	750 Abbasid caliphate established at Baghdad	711–13 Muslims conquer Samarkand and Indus Valley
757–96 Reign of Offa of Mercia	732 Charles Martel defeats Arabs at Poitiers		794 Japanese capital moves to Kyoto
865 Danes overrun East Anglia, Northumbria, and Eastern Mercia	800 Charlemagne crowned	969 Fatimids conquer Egypt	?960– Sung dynasty in China 1280
871–99 Reign of Alfred of Wessex	843 Partition of Charlemagne's empire	1055 Seljuk Turks capture Baghdad	*c.*1000 Greenland Vikings reach America
899–939 Wessex kings reconquer Danelaw	886 Vikings besiege Paris	1071 Seljuks defeat Byzantine army	
1016–35 Reign of Cnut	911 Vikings granted Duchy of Normandy	1096–99 First Crusade; Kingdom of Jerusalem established	
1066 Norman Conquest	962 Otto I crowned emperor at Rome		
1086 Domesday Survey	1054 Break between Greek and Latin churches	1187 Saladin overruns Kingdom of Jerusalem	
1170 Thomas à Becket murdered	1073–85 Quarrel between Holy Roman Empire and Papacy begins		1206 Sultanate of Delhi founded. Temujin (Genghis Khan) unites Mongol tribes
1215 Magna Carta	1202–4 Philip II of France captures Normandy and Anjou	1250 Mamluks seize power in Egypt	
1264–5 Baron's War against Henry III; Simon de Montfort killed		1258 Mongols sack Baghdad	
		1260 Mamluks defeat Mongols at Ain Jalut	1206–80 Mongol conquests

BRITAIN	EUROPE	ASIA AND AFRICA	AMERICA AND AUSTRALASIA
1277–83 Edward I annexes the Principality of Wales		1271–95 Travels of Marco Polo	
1296–1336 Anglo-Scottish Wars		c.1300 Ottoman Turkish expansion begins	c.1325–1520 Aztec civilization in Mexico
1327 Edward II deposed and murdered	1309–78 Papacy at Avignon	1368–1644 Ming dynasty in China	
1348 Black Death in England	1337 Beginning of Hundred Years' War in France	1380–1405 Career and conquests of Timur (Tamerlane)	c.1400–1525 Inca civilization in Andes
1381 Peasants' Revolt	1347–50 Black Death		
1399 Richard II deposed. Henry IV establishes Lancastrian dynasty			
1455–85 The Wars of the Roses	c.1450 Gutenberg starts printing		
	1450–53 English driven out of France		
	1453 Constantinople falls to Ottoman Turks		
	1462–1505 Reign of Ivan III	1486–98 Voyages of Bartolomeu Dias and Vasco da Gama	
1529–39 Henry VIII's Reformation Parliament and dissolution of the monasteries	1521 Condemnation of Martin Luther. Beginning of Protestantism	c.1500–1870 African slave trade	1492 Columbus reaches America
	1526 Turks overrun Hungary	1522–1680 Mughal expansion in India	1519 Cortes begins conquest of Aztec Empire
1554–58 Brief Catholic restoration under Mary Tudor		c.1550–c.1650 Russians colonize Siberia	1532 Pizarro begins conquest of Inca Empire
1588 Spanish Armada dispersed		1619 Dutch found Batavia (Djakarta)	1608 French colonists found Quebec
c.1590–c.1613 Shakespeare writes his plays and sonnets	c.1600–1650 Scientific work of Kepler, Galileo and Descartes	1630s Japan isolates itself from rest of world	1620 Mayflower puritans (Pilgrim Fathers) settle in New England
1603 James VI of Scotland succeeds to English throne	1618–48 Thirty Years' War		
	1643–1715 Reign of Louis XIV	1644–1911 Manchu dynasty in China	1645 Tasman discovers New Zealand
1642–48 Civil wars in England		1652 Dutch found Cape Colony	
1649 Charles I executed	1682–1725 Reign of Peter the Great, Tsar of Russia		
1660 Monarchy restored under Charles II	1740–86 Reign of Frederick the Great, King of Prussia		
1688 James II deposed	1756–63 Seven Years' War		
1707 Union of England and Scotland	1789 French Revolution begins	1757 Battle of Plassey; British defeat French in India	1776 American Declaration of Independence
c.1730 Wesley brothers found Methodism	1799 Napoleon seizes power in France		1788 British colony founded at Botany Bay, Australia
1800 Union of England and Ireland	1815 Battle of Waterloo; Congress of Vienna	1805 Beginning of East India Company's dominance in India	1817–24 Careers of Simon Bolivar and José de San Martin
1825 Stockton-Darlington railway completed	1821–29 Greek War of Liberation		
1845 Irish famine	1848 Year of revolutions throughout Europe	1839–42 Opium War; Britain takes Hong Kong	1840 Britain annexes New Zealand
1851 Great Exhibition, London	1854–6 Crimean War	1857–9 Indian Mutiny	1846–48 USA-Mexico War
1863 First London underground built. Darwin's Origin of the Species	1870–71 Franco-Prussian War	1869 Suez Canal opened	1861–65 American Civil War
	1885–95 Daimler and Benz work on automobile; Marconi's wireless	1880s 'Scramble for Africa';	1869 First trans-continental railway completed in USA
	1914 World War I begins	1900 Boxer Rebellion in China	1876 Alexander Bell patents telephone
	1917 Bolshevik revolution in Russia begins	1899–1902 Boer War	1898 Spanish-American War
1922 Irish Free State established	1922 Mussolini takes power in Italy	1911 Republic established in China under Sun Yat-sen	1903 Wright brothers: first powered flight
1926 General Strike	1933 Hitler becomes German Chancellor	1920–38 Career of Mustapha Kemal, Atatürk	1911 Mexican Revolution
	1936–39 Spanish Civil War	1937 Japan invades China	1914 Panama Canal opened
1940 Battle of Britain	1939 World War II begins	1941 Japanese attack Pearl Harbor	1929 Wall Street Crash begins Great Depression
	1941 Germany invades USSR	1945 USA drops atomic bombs on Japan	1941 USA enters Second World War
	1945 Defeat of Germany. Cold War begins	1947 India obtains independence	
	1957 USSR launches first space satellite. Treaty of Rome: formation of European Economic Community	1948 State of Israel founded	1959 Cuban Revolution
		1949 Communist victory in China.	1963 President Kennedy assassinated
1973 Britain enters European Economic Community		1952–80 African states win independence	1969 Neil Armstrong lands on the Moon
			1981 First Space shuttle

Reference Tables

MAJOR WARS

Date	Name	Won by	Against
431–404BC	Peloponnesian War	Peloponnesian League, led by Sparta, Corinth	Delian League, led by Athens
264–146BC	Punic Wars	Rome	Carthage
1337–1453	Hundred Years' War	France	England
1455–1485	Wars of the Roses	House of Lancaster	House of York
1618–1648	Thirty Years' War	France, Sweden, German Protestant states	The Holy Roman Empire, Spain
1642–1648	English Civil War	Parliament	Charles I
1701–1713	War of the Spanish Succession	England, Austria, Prussia, Netherlands	France, Bavaria, Cologne, Mantua, Savoy
1740–1748	War of the Austrian Succession	Austria, Hungary, Britain, Holland	Bavaria, France, Poland, Prussia, Sardinia, Saxony, Spain
1756–1763	Seven Years' War	Britain, Prussia, Hanover	Austria, France, Russia, Sweden
1775–1783	American War of Independence	Thirteen Colonies	Britain
1792–1815	Napoleonic Wars	Austria, Britain, Prussia, Russia, Spain, Sweden	France
1812–1814	War of 1812	United States	Britain
1846–1848	Mexican-American War	United States	Mexico
1854–1856	Crimean War	Britain, France, Sardinia, Turkey	Russia
1861–1865	American Civil War	23 Northern States (the Union)	11 Southern States (the Confederacy)
1870–1871	Franco-Prussian War	Prussia and other German states	France
1894–1895	Chinese-Japanese War (1st)	Japan	China
1898	Spanish-American War	United States	Spain
1899–1902	Boer (South African) War	Britain	Boer Republics
1904–1905	Russo-Japanese War	Japan	Russia
1914–1918	First World War	Belgium, Britain and Empire, France, Italy, Japan, Russia, Serbia, United States	Austria-Hungary, Bulgaria, Germany, Ottoman Empire
1931–1933	Chinese-Japanese War (2nd)	Japan	China
1935–1936	Abyssinian War	Italy	Abyssinia (Ethiopia)
1936–1939	Spanish Civil War	Junta de Defensa Nacional (Fascists)	Republican government
1937–1945	Chinese-Japanese War (3rd)	China	Japan
1939–1945	Second World War	Australia, Belgium, Britain, Canada, China, Denmark, France, Greece, Netherlands, New Zealand, Norway, Poland, Russia, South Africa, United States, Yugoslavia	Bulgaria, Finland, Germany, Hungary, Italy, Japan, Romania
1950–1953	Korean War	South Korea and United Nations forces	North Korea and Chinese forces
1957–1975	Vietnam War	North Vietnam	South Vietnam, United States
1967	Six-Day War	Israel	Egypt, Syria, Jordan, Iraq
1967–1970	Nigerian Civil War	Federal Government	Biafra
1971	Pakistani Civil War	East Pakistan (Bangladesh) and India	West Pakistan
1973	Yom Kippur War	Ceasefire arranged by United Nations: fought by Israel against Egypt, Syria, Iraq, Jordan, Sudan, Saudi Arabia, Lebanon	

MAJOR BATTLES

GREEKS AND ROMANS
Marathon 490BC Force of 10,000 Athenians and allies defeated 50,000 Persian troops, crushing a Persian invasion attempt.
Salamis 480BC Greek fleet of 360 ships defeated Persian fleet of 1000 ships. Persians had to withdraw from Greece.
Arbela 331BC Alexander the Great's Greek army defeated a Persian force twice the size and conquered Persia.
Actium 31BC Roman fleet of 400 ships under Octavian (later Emperor Augustus) defeated 500 ships, the combined fleet of Mark Antony and Cleopatra.
Châlons-sur-Marne 451 Romans and Visigoths defeated the Huns led by Attila.

EARLY EUROPE
Tours 732 The Franks under Charles Martel defeated the Saracens (Muslims), halting their advance in western Europe.
Lech 955 Emperor Otto the Great ended the Magyar threat in western Europe.
Hastings 1066 About 8000 troops under Duke William of Normandy defeated an equal force under Saxon king Harold II. England soon came under Norman rule.
Crécy 1346 Invading army of 10,000 English defeated 20,000 French. English archers won the day.
Agincourt 1415 Henry V of England with 10,000 troops defeated 30,000 Frenchmen and recaptured Normandy.
Siege of Orléans 1428–1429 English troops began siege in October 1428 but in April 1429 Joan of Arc came to the aid of the city and forced the besiegers to withdraw.
Siege of Constantinople 1453 Ottoman Turkish army of more than 100,000 captured the city, held by 10,000 men.

WARS OF FAITH AND SUCCESSION
Lepanto 1571 Allied Christian fleet of 208 galleys defeated Ali Pasha's Turkish fleet of 230 galleys.
Armada 1588 Spanish invasion fleet defeated by the English.
Boyne 1690 William III of England with 35,000 troops routed his rival, James II, with 21,000 men.
Blenheim 1704 A British-Austrian army led by Duke of Marlborough and Prince Eugène defeated the French and Bavarians during the War of the Spanish Succession.

COLONIAL STRUGGLES
Plassey 1757 Robert Clive with an Anglo-Indian army of 3000 defeated the Nawab of Bengal's army of 60,000, conquering Bengal and setting Britain on the road to domination in India.
Quebec 1759 British troops under James Wolfe made a night attack up the St Lawrence River. They defeated the French forces under the Marquis de Montcalm. Montcalm and Wolfe were killed.

Yorktown 1781 8000 British troops surrendered to a larger force under George Washington. American War of Independence ended.

AGE OF NAPOLEON
Trafalgar 1805 British fleet of 27 ships under Nelson shattered Franco-Spanish fleet of 33 ships. Nelson was killed. Napoleon's hopes of invading England ended.
Austerlitz 1805 Emperor Napoleon I with 65,000 French troops defeated an 83,000-strong Austro-Russian army under the Austrian and Russian Emperors.
Jena and Auerstädt 1806 French forces routed the main Prussian armies on the same day (October 14), shattering Prussian power.
Waterloo 1815 A British, Dutch, and Belgian force of 67,000 fought off 74,000 French troops under Napoleon I until the arrival of Blücher's Prussian army. It ended Napoleon's final bid for power.

FIRST WORLD WAR
Marne 1914 French and British armies halted German forces invading France.
First battle of Ypres 1914 German forces trying to reach Calais lost 150,000 men. British and French forces held off attack, losing more than 100,000 men.
Verdun 1916 In a six-month struggle French forces held off a major attack by German armies. French losses were 348,000; German losses 328,000.
Jutland 1916 British Grand Fleet fought German High Seas Fleet. The Germans did not again venture out to sea.
Somme 1916 In a 141-day battle following Verdun, the British and French captured 320 sq km (125 sq miles) of ground, losing 600,000 men. The German defenders lost almost 500,000 men.
Passchendaele 1917 British forces launched eight attacks over 102 days in heavy rain and through thick mud. They gained 8 km (5 miles) and lost 400,000 men.

SECOND WORLD WAR
Britain 1940 A German air force of 2500 planes launched an attack lasting 114 days to try and win air supremacy over Britain. The smaller Royal Air Force defeated the attack.
Midway 1942 A fleet of 100 Japanese ships was defeated in the Pacific by an American fleet half the size.
El Alamein 1942 Montgomery's British Eighth Army drove Rommel's German Afrika Korps out of Egypt and deep into Libya.
Stalingrad 1942–1943 Twenty-one German divisions tried to capture Stalingrad (now Volgograd) but siege was broken and more than 100,000 German troops surrendered.
Normandy 1944 Allied forces under Eisenhower invaded German-held northern France in biggest-ever sea-borne attack. After a month of fighting Germans retreated.
Leyte Gulf 1944 United States 3rd and 7th fleets defeated a Japanese force, ending Japanese naval power in World War II.
Ardennes Bulge 1944–1945 Last German counter-attack in west through Ardennes Forest failed. Germans lost 100,000 casualties and 110,000 prisoners.

FAMOUS ROMAN EMPERORS

	Reigned		Reigned
Augustus (Octavian)	27BC–AD14	Diocletian	284–305
Tiberus	14–37	Maximian	286–305
Caligula (Gaius)	37–41	Constantine the Great	311–337
Claudius	41–54		
Nero	54–68	Valentinian I (in the West)	364–375
		Valens (in the East)	364–378
Vespasian	69–79		
Titus	79–81	Theodosius, the Great (in the East, and after 394, in the West)	379–395
Trajan	98–117		
Hadrian	117–138		
Antoninus Pius	138–161	Honorius (in the West)	395–423
Marcus Aurelius	161–180		
		Theodosius II (in the East)	408–450
Septimius Severus	193–211	Valentinian III (in the West)	425–455
Alexander Severus	222–235	Zeno (in the East)	474–491
		Romulus Augustulus (in the West)	475–476
Valerian	253–259		

HOLY ROMAN EMPERORS

FRANKISH KINGS AND EMPERORS (CAROLINGIAN)

	Reigned
Charlemagne	800–814
Louis I, the Pious	814–840
Lothair I	840–855
Louis II	855–875
Charles II, the Bald	875–877
Throne vacant	877–881
Charles III, the Fat	881–887
Throne vacant	887–891
Guido of Spoleto	891–894
Lambert of Spoleto (co-emperor)	892–898
Arnulf (rival)	896–901
Louis III of Provence	901–905
Berengar	905–924
Conrad I of Franconia (rival)	911–918

SAXON KINGS AND EMPERORS

Henry I, the Fowler	918–936
Otto I, the Great	936–973
Otto II	973–983
Otto III	983–1002
Henry II, the Saint	1002–1024

FRANCONIAN EMPERORS (SALIAN)

Conrad II, the Salian	1024–1039
Henry III, the Black	1039–1056
Henry IV	1056–1106
Rudolf of Swabia (rival)	1077–1080
Hermann of Luxemburg (rival)	1081–1093
Conrad of Franconia (rival)	1093–1101
Henry V	1106–1125
Lothair II	1125–1137

HOHENSTAUFEN KINGS AND EMPERORS

Conrad III	1138–1152
Frederick I Barbarossa	1152–1190
Henry VI	1190–1197
Otto IV	1198–1215
Philip of Swabia (rival)	1198–1208
Frederick II	1215–1250

	Reigned
Henry Raspe (rival)	1246–1247
William of Holland (rival)	1247–1256
Conrad IV	1250–1254
The Great Interregnum	1254–1273

RULERS FROM DIFFERENT HOUSES

Richard of Cornwall (rival)	1257–1272
Alfonso X of Castile (rival)	1257–1273
Rudolf I, Habsburg	1273–1291
Adolf I of Nassau	1292–1298
Albert I, Habsburg	1298–1308
Henry VII, Luxemburg	1308–1313
Louis IV of Bavaria	1314–1347
Frederick of Habsburg (co-regent)	1314–1325
Charles IV, Luxemburg	1347–1378
Wenceslas of Bohemia	1378–1400
Frederick III of Brunswick	1400
Rupert of the Palatinate	1400–1410
Sigismund, Luxemburg	1410–1437

HABSBURG EMPERORS

Albert II	1438–1439
Frederick III	1440–1493
Maximilian I	1493–1519
Charles V	1519–1558
Ferdinand I	1558–1564
Maximilian II	1564–1576
Rudolf II	1576–1612
Matthias	1612–1619
Ferdinand II	1619–1637
Ferdinand III	1637–1657
Leopold I	1658–1705
Joseph I	1705–1711
Charles VI	1711–1740
Charles VII of Bavaria	1742–1745

HABSBURG-LORRAINE EMPERORS

Francis I of Lorraine	1745–1765
Joseph II	1765–1790
Leopold II	1790–1792
Francis II	1792–1806

BRITISH RULERS

Rulers of England (to 1603)

Saxons

Egbert	827–839
Ethelwulf	839–858
Ethelbald	858–860
Ethelbert	860–865
Ethelred I	865–871
Alfred the Great	871–899
Edward the Elder	899–924
Athelstan	924–939
Edmund	939–946
Edred	946–955
Edwy	955–959
Edgar	959–975
Edward the Martyr	975–978
Ethelred II the Unready	978–1016
Edmund Ironside	1016

Danes

Canute	1016–1035
Harold I Harefoot	1035–1040
Hardicanute	1040–1042

Saxons

Edward the Confessor	1042–1066
Harold II	1066

House of Normandy

William I the Conqueror	1066–1087
William II	1087–1100
Henry I	1100–1135
Stephen	1135–1154

House of Plantagenet

Henry II	1154–1189
Richard I	1189–1199
John	1199–1216
Henry III	1216–1272
Edward I	1272–1307
Edward II	1307–1327
Edward III	1327–1377
Richard II	1377–1399

House of Lancaster

Henry IV	1399–1413
Henry V	1413–1422
Henry VI	1422–1461

House of York

Edward IV	1461–1483
Edward V	1483
Richard III	1483–1485

House of Tudor

Henry VII	1485–1509
Henry VIII	1509–1547
Edward VI	1547–1553
Mary I	1553–1558
Elizabeth I	1558–1603

Rulers of Scotland (to 1603)

Malcolm II	1005–1034
Dunclan I	1034–1040
Macbeth	1040–1057
Malcolm III Canmore	1058–1093
Donald Bane	1093–1094
Duncan II	1094
Donald Bane (restored)	1094–1097
Edgar	1097–1107
Alexander I	1107–1124
David I	1124–1153
Malcolm IV	1153–1165
William the Lion	1165–1214
Alexander II	1214–1249
Alexander III	1249–1286
Margaret of Norway	1286–1290
John Baliol	1292–1296
Robert I (Bruce)	1306–1329
David II	1329–1371

House of Stuart

Robert II	1371–1390
Robert III	1390–1406
James I	1406–1437
James II	1437–1460
James III	1460–1488
James IV	1488–1513
James V	1513–1542
Mary	1542–1567
James VI (James I of England)	1567–1625

Rulers of Britain

House of Stuart

James I	1603–1625
Charles I	1625–1649
Commonwealth	1649–1660
Charles II	1660–1685
James II	1685–1688
William III	1689–1702
Mary II	1689–1694 } jointly
Anne	1702–1714

House of Hanover

George I	1714–1727
George II	1727–1760
George III	1760–1820
George IV	1820–1830
William IV	1830–1837
Victoria	1837–1901

House of Saxe-Coburg

Edward VII	1901–1910

House of Windsor

George V	1910–1936
Edward VIII	1936
George VI	1936–1952
Elizabeth II	1952–

AMERICAN PRESIDENTS

F = Federalist; DR = Democratic-Republican; D = Democratic; W = Whig; R = Republican; U = Union

		Term
1	George Washington (F)	1789–1797
2	John Adams (F)	1797–1801
3	Thomas Jefferson (DR)	1801–1809
4	James Madison (DR)	1809–1817
5	James Monroe (DR)	1817–1825
6	John Quincy Adams (DR)	1825–1829
7	Andrew Jackson (D)	1829–1837
8	Martin Van Buren (D)	1837–1841
9	William H. Harrison* (W)	1841
10	John Tyler (W)	1841–1845
11	James K. Polk (D)	1845–1849
12	Zachary Taylor* (W)	1849–1850
13	Millard Fillmore (W)	1850–1853
14	Franklin Pierce (D)	1853–1857
15	James Buchanan (D)	1857–1861
16	Abraham Lincoln† (R)	1861–1865
17	Andrew Johnson (U)	1865–1869
18	Ulysses S. Grant (R)	1869–1877
19	Rutherford B. Hayes (R)	1877–1881
20	James A. Garfield† (R)	1881
21	Chester A. Arthur (R)	1881–1885
22	Grover Cleveland (D)	1885–1889
23	Benjamin Harrison (D)	1889–1893
24	Grover Cleveland (D)	1893–1897
25	William McKinley† (R)	1897–1901
26	Theodore Roosevelt (R)	1901–1909
27	William H. Taft (R)	1909–1913
28	Woodrow Wilson (D)	1913–1921
29	Warren G. Harding* (R)	1921–1923
30	Calvin Coolidge (R)	1923–1929
31	Herbert C. Hoover (R)	1929–1933
32	Franklin D. Roosevelt* (D)	1933–1945
33	Harry S. Truman (D)	1945–1953
34	Dwight D. Eisenhower (R)	1953–1961
35	John F. Kennedy† (D)	1961–1963
36	Lyndon B. Johnson (D)	1963–1969
37	Richard M. Nixon (R)	1969–1974
38	Gerald R. Ford (R)	1974–1977
39	Jimmy Carter (D)	1977–1981
40	Ronald Reagan (R)	1981–

*Died in office
†Assassinated in office

RULERS OF FRANCE

Hugh Capet	987–996	John I	1316	Charles IX	1560–1574
Robert II, the Pious	996–1031	Philip V	1316–1322	Henri III	1574–1589
Henri I	1031–1060	Charles IV	1322–1328	Henri IV	1589–1610
Philip I	1060–1108	Philip VI	1328–1350	Louis XIII	1610–1643
Louis VI, the Fat	1108–1137	John II	1350–1364	Louis XIV	1643–1715
Louis VII, the Young	1137–1180	Charles V	1364–1380	Louis XV	1715–1774
Philip II Augustus	1180–1223	Charles VI	1380–1422	Louis XVI	1774–1792
Louis VIII	1223–1226	Charles VII	1422–1461	*The First Republic*	1792–1804
Louis IX, Saint Louis	1226–1270	Louis XI	1461–1483	Napoleon I (Emperor)	1804–1814
Philip III, the Bold	1270–1285	Charles VIII	1483–1498	Louis XVIII	1814–1824
Philip IV, the Fair	1285–1314	Louis XII	1498–1515	Charles X	1824–1830
Louis X	1314–1316	François I	1515–1547	Louis Philippe	1830–1848
		Henri II	1547–1559	*The Second Republic*	1848–1852
		François II	1559–1560	Napoleon III (Emperor)	1852–1870

Index

ACKNOWLEDGEMENTS

Endpapers Michael Holford; title page British Museum; 6 top British Museum, bottom ZEFA; 7 top SCALA; 8 Sonia Halliday; 9 top ZEFA, bottom NASA; 12 French Government Tourist Office; 13 British Museum; 14 top ZEFA, bottom SCALA; 15 bottom British Museum; 17 top British Museum, bottom right Brooklyn Museum; 18 top Sonia Halliday, bottom Ronald Sheridan; 19 bottom Sonia Halliday; 21 bottom SCALA; 22 bottom ZEFA; 23 British Museum; 25 left British Museum, right Metropolitan Museum of Art, Fletcher Fund 1934; 26, 27 Ronald Sheridan; 28 top British Museum, bottom Michael Holford; 33 top Walters Art Gallery, Baltimore; 34 bottom British Museum; 35 bottom Sonia Halliday; 36 bottom Sonia Halliday; 37 bottom Bibliothèque Nationale; 39 Giraudon, Paris; 41 Alan Hutchison; 42 British Museum; 43 bottom Mansell Collection; 44 British Museum; 48 bottom Michael Holford; 50 top British Museum, bottom Cooper-Bridgeman Library; 52 SCALA; 53 top SCALA, centre British Museum; 57 top National Army Museum, bottom ZEFA; 62 bottom Mansell Collection; 63 bottom Mansell Collection; 64 South American Pictures; 65 bottom Library of Congress; 66 top, centre Mansell Collection, bottom Mary Evans Picture Library; 69 top National Army Museum, bottom Lent by Kyoto Costume Institute; 70 top Mary Evans Picture Library, bottom Michael Holford; 71 bottom Syndication International; 74 F.A.O.; 75 top United Nations, bottom Red Cross, Geneva; 77 top Peter Newark, bottom Alan Hutchison; 78 bottom Vision International/Paola Koch; 79 top Frank Spooner Pictures; 81 top ZEFA, bottom Alan Hutchison.

nais.

Mare germanic

Tera del Rey de portugall

Os montes claros en affrica

Carabos   Castello damina.

Esta he conosso Sanctae castella. 7 portuguall

Mareoccanus.

Follus antarnais.